Building and Equipping The
GARDEN AND SMALL
FARM WORKSHOP

BUILDING AND EQUIPPING THE GARDEN AND SMALL FARM WORKSHOP

Monte Burch

GARDEN WAY PUBLISHING

CHARLOTTE, VERMONT 05445

Library of Congress Cataloging in Publication Data

Burch, Monte.
  Building and equipping the garden and small farm
workshop.

  Includes index.
  1. Workshops.   2. Farm shops.   I. Title.
II. Title: Garden and small farm workshop.
TT152.B87   631.3'04   79-20721
ISBN 0-88266-156-6

Acknowledgments

I would like to thank *Workbench, Family Handyman* and *How-To* magazines for allowing me to use material previously used in those magazines.

I would also like to thank the following companies for providing photos, materials or just plain good advice and information.

Belsaw Co.
Bernz-O-Matic Corp.
Brownell's Inc.
Crescent Tool Co.
Garden Way Mfg. Co. Inc.
Indian Ridge Traders Inc.
Jacobsen Mfg. Co.
Knape & Vogt Mfg. Co.
Lincoln Electric Co.
Lufkin Division, Cooper Industries
McCulloch Corp.
Miller Falls Co.
Power Tool Institute
Rockwell International
Sears, Roebuck & Co., Power Tool
    Division
Shop Smith, Inc.
Stanley Tool Works
Vaughan & Bushnell Mfg. Co.
White Motor Corp.

Contents

Chapter 1

The Workshop

The homestead workshop is a very personal thing. To some, it might be a section of a garage that has a workbench and a few tools. To others, a garden or small farm workshop might be a separate building with woodworking and metalworking tools and perhaps an area for crafts such as leatherworking or pottery.

The design depends on what the person uses the workshop for. And workshops can be large or small, filled with tools, or just bare necessities. You don't have to have a large, elaborate shop for most garden and small farm repair or building jobs.

For example, a great uncle of mine had a small shop in an old shed by his back door. It was run-down, had a leaky roof, and dirt floor; one end was completely open; and there was no heat or light. An old hand-hewn workbench was always littered with hand-made tools. From this simple little shop he turned out beautiful chairs made of native wood. As you can guess, he worked only during the warm days of summer and good weather, and since his backstep was nearby he did a lot of work sitting on his steps. From this same shop also came beautiful plaited leather whips as well as hand-made hunting and kitchen knives. He spent the latter part of his life building beautiful items and raising hunting dogs and trapping, and he made a fair living selling the results.

The main requirements for a workshop are adequate workspace and a place to store and protect tools and materials. It should also have enough natural light so you can work without having to turn on an electric light and should be well ventilated for such chores as spraying finishes or welding.

LEAN TO. A good first small workshop is a small lean-to built against the side of a house or barn. This is convenient and saves materials because you can use one side of an existing building. A lean-to is also easier to construct than a free standing unit. A free-standing, separate building does, however, have advantages. For one thing, it's safer—you can store flammable items or do chores such as welding without worrying about possibly losing a house or barn.

I have seen workshops in barns, garages, basements, and even apartment kitchens. Each was a very personal workshop.

STORAGE UNIT. If you are limited by space or funds, one solution is to build a small tool storage shed. The tools can be carried outside and used during warm weather in front of the workshop. Later you can add an awning or shelter to the front to work under during hot days or bad weather. If necessary, you can enclose the sides to construct a full-size workshop.

PLANS. Shown are plans, with several views, for two different workshops: a small, free-standing shop, with and without an addition; and a full-size shop that can also be used as a garage, or machine shed. If you're involved in farm operations, you may wish to make your shop large enough so you can pull a tractor or other equipment inside for repairs during bad weather.

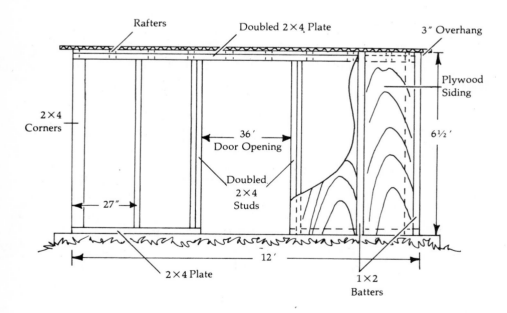

This small, free-standing shop (front view) may be made with standard-size lumber, a wood or corrugated-metal roof and concrete slab foundation.

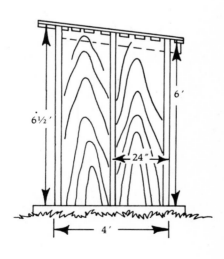

Side view of the free-standing shop, without expansion or addition.

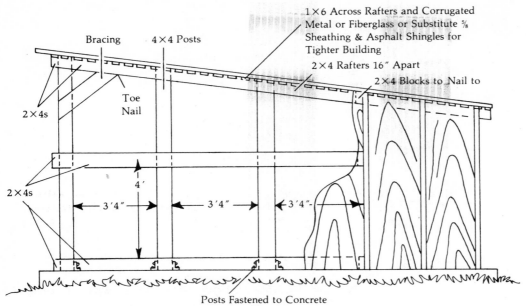

Bracing 4×4 Posts

1×6 Across Rafters and Corrugated
Metal or Fiberglass or Substitute ⅝
Sheathing & Asphalt Shingles for
Tighter Building

2×4 Rafters 16″ Apart

2×4 Blocks to Nail to

Toe Nail

2×4s

2×4s

4′

3′4″   3′4″   3′4″

Posts Fastened to Concrete
Pad With Angle Irons

Free-standing shop with addition.

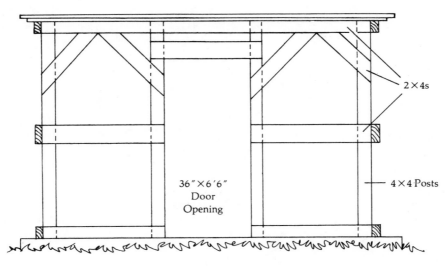

2×4s

36″×6′6″
Door
Opening

4×4 Posts

Free-standing shop with addition (front view).

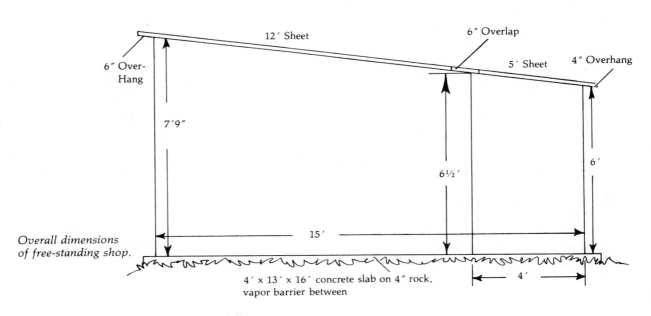

12′ Sheet   6″ Overlap

6″ Over-Hang

5′ Sheet   4″ Overhang

7′9″

6½′

6′

15′

4′

Overall dimensions of free-standing shop.

4′ x 13′ x 16′ concrete slab on 4″ rock,
vapor barrier between

Free-standing shop with en-closed addition. Details and di-mensions remain the same as those shown on page 3. Ends are trimmed with 1 x 4s.

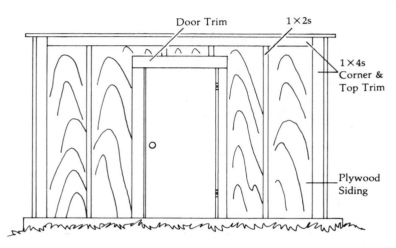

Door Trim

1×2s

1×4s Corner & Top Trim

Plywood Siding

Enclosed, free-standing shop (front view).

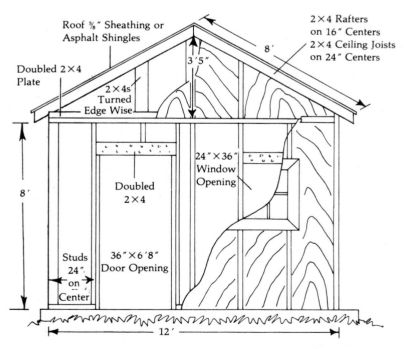

Roof ⅝" Sheathing or Asphalt Shingles

2×4 Rafters on 16" Centers
2×4 Ceiling Joists on 24" Centers

Doubled 2×4 Plate

2×4s Turned Edge Wise

3′5″

8′

8′

Doubled 2×4

24″×36″ Window Opening

Studs 24″ on Center

36″×6′8″ Door Opening

12′

Basic plan for a full-sized, enclosed workshop, with a 12'6" x 16'6" concrete pad foundation. The shop may be built to a length of 15' with a 1' roof overhang on each end.

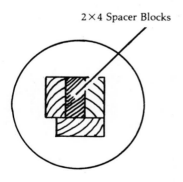

2×4 Spacer Blocks

Detailed, bird's-eye view of the corner framing used in the shop. Corners are made of 2 x 4s arranged as shown.

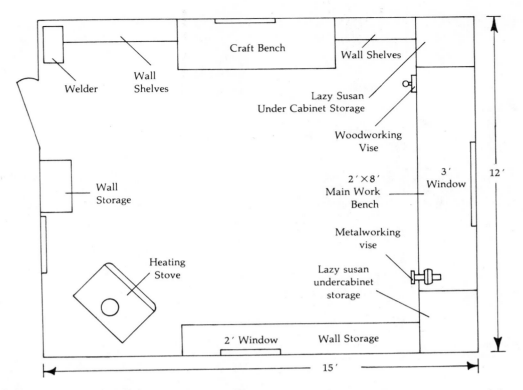

Before building your shop, make a working drawing of the floor plan, keeping in mind the room you'll need for projects, tools and equipment. It's a good idea to locate the workbench near a north-facing window to avoid direct sun glare.

LAYOUT. The size or structure of your workshop isn't as important as how you lay it out. Arrange the shop to suit your needs, keeping the efficient use of space in mind.

When planning your shop, determine how you will use it and what you will need in the way of working space, tool and material storage. It's a good idea to get a scale ruler and make a small-scale sketch of your shop. You can then figure how to best arrange the shop. Your alternatives will be determined by the stationary power tools you will have, if any, and whether you will include welding, metal working sections and any other craft areas, in addition to the regular tool and work space used for repairing or building items.

You may also wish to provide space in the shop to store things such as rakes, hoes, even a lawn mower and small garden tractor.

WORKBENCH. Planning placement of the workbench is most important. This is where you will be doing the most work and the bench should be located accordingly. Ideally, it should be centrally located and within easy reach of the other shop areas such as tool and material storage. Ideally, the workbench would be located next to a north-facing window. This provides plenty of light, without glare.

The workbench should have at least one corner free for a vise. If a vise is placed near a wall you won't be able to get long materials in it. If possible, both ends of the bench should be free, then you can locate a woodworking vise on one end and a heavy-duty metalworking vise on the opposite.

If it is not possible to locate the bench under a window, a good, strong light should be hung directly overhead. One of the best choices is a long fluorescent light which contains a reflector and can be hung from the ceiling with small chains or wire.

Ideally, your shop should include a workbench with a good woodworking vise and a metalworking vise on the opposite end.

POWER TOOLS. If you have stationary power tools they should be located so material can be fed into them easily. If you have a small shop, for instance, you can locate a radial arm saw right next to a door. Then, if necessary, long pieces can stick out the door. Or you may wish to add a garage door on the front of the shop. By opening this, long pieces can be handled in a small shop easily and stationary power tools can be rolled out next to the opening for easier use.

SPECIFICATIONS. Although a shop can have a dirt floor, the best bet is a concrete or, even better yet, wooden floor. Wood is easier to stand on for long hours, but it's more expensive than concrete and takes more time to build. The usual floor and shop foundation is a poured concrete pad. Heavy tools may be rolled around on this floor; it also keeps the shop warmer and drier than a dirt floor.

If you have different types of work such as woodworking and leatherworking, make a small separate area for each, and keep each craft separate. This makes it easier to identify tools and generally avoids confusion.

The ceiling height is also important. Although a low ceiling will make it easier to heat the shop in wintertime, it also makes it a bit harder to handle long materials.

Storage of materials is also important. In most cases, a rack built outside along the shop and covered with a small roof is the best choice for material storage except for fine woods, or plywoods which must be stored in a dry place to keep them from separating.

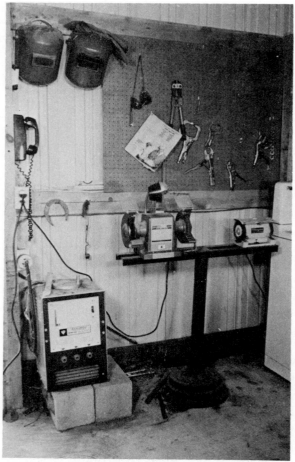

Craft areas for leatherworking, pottery, soldering and similar activities should be separated from the rest of the shop if possible.

6

The Workbench

The workbench is probably the single most important item in your shop. A workbench can be anything from a couple of boards laid over two sawhorses to an elaborate affair with drawers for tools, and all kinds of vises and holding devices. Only one thing, however, is important: height. Many folks have workbenches too low to work at comfortably. After an hour or two, bending over a low workbench, your back hurts so bad you don't feel like doing any work. The workbench height should be adjusted to suit your stature. Normally, this would be about 30 to 36 inches high.

The bench should be 22 to 30 inches wide. Any wider and it is hard to reach items on the back or on the wall behind the bench. Any narrower and you won't have a wide enough work space. The length of the bench can be a matter of choice; a six- to eight-foot bench provides the best working space. For those with limited space a four-foot long bench may be necessary.

As mentioned before, the best bet is to attach a woodworking vise on one end of the bench and a metalworking vise on the opposite. The second most important part of the workbench is the top. This should be made of sturdy two-inch thick material to provide a heavy-duty work space. My favorite workbench top is made of 2 × 6s, covered with a piece of ⅛-inch hardboard. The hardboard provides a good smooth working surface and if it becomes mangled with holes or covered with paint or glue, you can merely remove the hardboard covering and replace it with a new one.

The underside of the workbench can be left open and the bracing used as a shelf to hold materials or long tools. Or you can enclose the underside, making it a cabinet with doors and a drawer to hold tools and materials.

Drawers should be built so their dimensions—especially the depth—are appro-

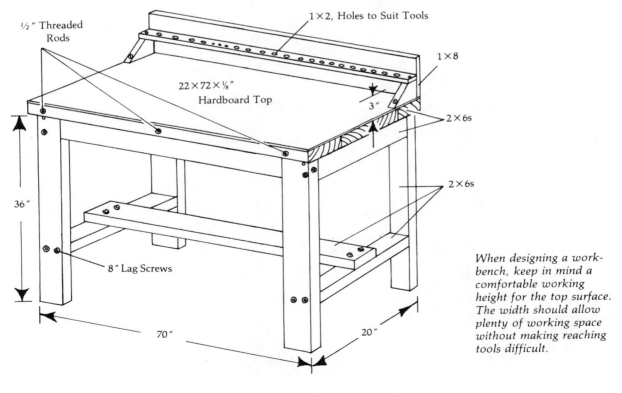

When designing a workbench, keep in mind a comfortable working height for the top surface. The width should allow plenty of working space without making reaching tools difficult.

priate for the tools to be placed in them. Then you won't end up with a deep drawer full of tools and have to dig through them to get to those you need. This is frustrating, and can injure you and damage tools. The bench drawers can be used for tools you may not use frequently, such as planes and carving gouges.

The workbench, regardless of its type or style, should be sturdy and well anchored to the wall and floor. Nothing is more frustrating than trying to saw a pipe or a piece of wood on a workbench that shakes and wobbles all over the place.

It's a good idea to provide additional tool storage along the back wall behind the bench. This can be for tools you will use often such as hammers, saws, screwdrivers and punches. It's also handy to have a tool box that can be carried around the farm for on-the-job repairs. Mechanics' tools can be stored in home-made chests with casters that can be rolled about the workshop. Or, these tools can be hung on a wall.

Providing a storage cabinet for power tools is another good idea. Ideally, this should be with a small separate shelf or drawer for each tool and its accessories. This can be under the workbench or you may prefer to build a small separate cabinet. I have a small metal kitchen cabinet with built-in shelves in my shop. For power tool storage, it's perfect.

Electricity & Lighting

Electrical power, though not mandatory for small shops, is helpful. Not only does it drive power tools, including welders, but electric lights allow for nighttime work.

Check local electrical codes for rules on wiring a shop. In most instances, you will be required to run the shop wiring to a separate fuse or circuit breaker, whether the shop is attached to your house or barn, where the electrical service entrance is. A small shop with only a few power tools,

The back wall behind a workbench, fitted with a tool rack, provides plenty of space for most commonly used tools.

8

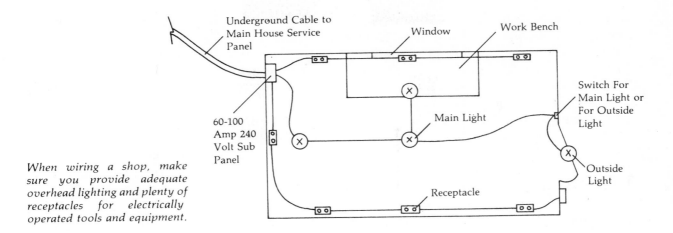

When wiring a shop, make sure you provide adequate overhead lighting and plenty of receptacles for electrically operated tools and equipment.

lights and plug-ins for portable electric tools can get by with a small box of about 60 amps, but with several power tools a 100-amp fuse or circuit breaker box is better. The cost will be greater initially but less in the long run.

When wiring a shop make sure you provide plenty of receptacles and that all are grounded. It's a good idea to provide a row of receptacles around the workbench, either behind, on the sides or front, because that is where you will most often be using a portable electric drill, soldering gun, and other electrical equipment. A strip receptacle is a good idea for the workbench because it provides more plug-ins. In addition, locate electrical receptacles about every six feet around the room. You may also wish to have a

grounded waterproof receptacle for work outside the shop. This circuit should also be protected by a ground fault interrupter.

In addition to the main light over the workbench you will also need a main light in the shop with a switch by the door. A two-way switch in the house, or a light outside the door and a switch in the house are convenient and permit trips between the house and the shop at night with a light.

There should also be a light over specific work areas such as a metalworking bench, drill press and radial arm saw. Each

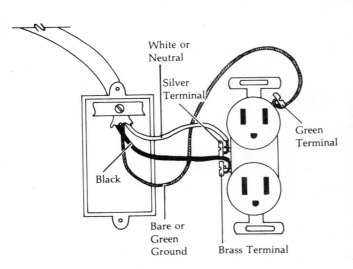

Grounded receptacle

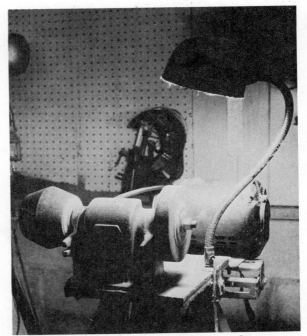

A clamp-on lamp is ideal for lighting individual tools and equipment.

9

of these lights should be located so it directs light down on the work and so that neither the tool nor you creates shadows. One answer is to use clamp-on lights that fit directly on the tool. These lights may be directed exactly where you want; and you don't have to use a large bulb to get good lighting on the work.

Heating

You may not wish to install heat in the shop, but if you don't you won't be able to store latex paint and several other items that freezing damages. A small shop can be heated easily with a small electrical space heater that can be turned on only while you are in the shop. This will knock the chill off all but the coldest winter days. In farm supply stores, these are often called "milk barn" heaters; they are also used to warm greenhouses. Another type of heater is the kerosene heater used by builders. This type uses kerosene and a fan and can heat large areas quickly, but it must have adequate ventilation or you can get poisoned by fumes.

The ideal choice for a small shop is a wood stove. But you might not be able to get any insurance coverage on the shop. (To be sure, check with your insurance agent.) Nothing, however, quite beats an old wood stove for heating a small shop quickly and conveniently. Just make sure it is kept well away from all walls, combustibles and flammable items. The stove should be mounted on bricks or metal asbestos pad. The flue pipe should be run through the wooden part of the building with caution and according to all safety rules. (Consult your local insurance agent or fire department for details.)

A small stove can be used to burn scraps from your woodworking projects, but remember that softwoods such as pine will soon coat the stove pipe with resin and pitch, which can result in a dangerous flue fire. Clean out the flue often.

Paint Room

Most large shops have a separate room for finishing or painting. The reason is that these activities, especially spray finishing,

No workshop should be without a fire extinguisher, especially if the shop is heated with a wood stove or if flammable materials are used.

10

are dangerous near any flame such as the pilot light of a furnace. So make sure the spray room or booth is well away from the rest of the shop and well ventilated. I do all spray finishing outside when possible, and, if not possible, I shut down all pilot lights and use a small fan to pull spraying fumes out of the shop.

You will also need paint and hardware shelves to hold jars of paint, finish, and other odds and ends that farm owners inevitably end up with.

Shelves can be made simply of 1 x 12s, either braced and nailed to the wall or laid across shelving hangers inserted in pegboard. Using hangers is the more expensive method.

If your shop is a combined shop and garden tool shed you may want to put racks and hangers on one wall for garden tools such as rakes and hoes, and make space to hang the garden tiller, shredder, and lawn mower.

There are several accessories you can build for your shop that will make working in it easy and enjoyable. Most can be built easily from scrap material left over from other jobs.

Sawhorses

There are almost as many variations of sawhorses as there are workshops, but whatever the design, sawhorses should be durable and sturdy. Ideally, they should be made in the same manner and have the same height. The height should be just right for you to place a piece of wood across them and hold it securely with your knee while sawing. Normally this will be about 22 inches high; however, you might wish to lower or raise the height to suit your stature. Shown is a typical old-time sawhorse. Although it is made of one-inch material except for the top piece, which is a 2 x 6, this sawhorse is sturdy due to the splayed legs.

This sawhorse also makes a handy step stool because it won't wobble or tip over easily and it's easy to carry.

Workstool

Another type of sawhorse is the handy workstool that serves as a combination small workbench, step stool, and sawhorse. The hand hold allows you easily to carry it to the job; and it is lightweight yet sturdy.

Bracket Sawhorses

The easiest sawhorses to make are simply 2 x 4 pieces cut and fit into purchased sawhorse brackets. These can be made with different heights for different jobs. A pair made extra tall can be coupled with a sheet of plywood to make a temporary table.

A typical sawhorse made of 1″ material, except for the top piece, which is a 2 x 6 (1½″ x 5½″). The legs may be made of 1 x 6s (¾″ x 5½″).

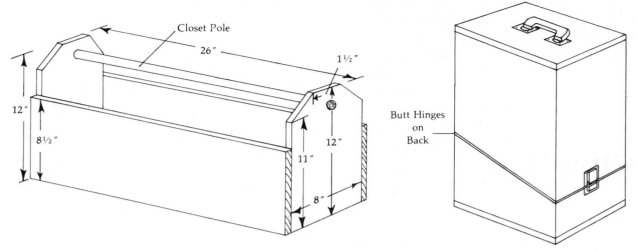

A toolbox may be built from 1 x 12" stock with dividers to suit the owner's tools. A router case may be made of the same material and sized appropriately.

Toolbox

If you do any work around the farm at all, sooner or later you'll need a tool box. Regardless of what tools I throw in the truck or stick in my pocket, as soon as I get away from the shop, down in the pig lot or some other place, I find that I'm missing a tool I need. My answer is a multi-purpose tool box suited to the farm. It has the most frequently used tools plus a few that you won't find in a city carpenter's box, for instance a hog ringer and box of hog rings. The ringer is used to put copper rings in a pig's nose to prevent the animal from rooting out of a pen.

The tool box has sections for different tools and a lift-out nail tray which carries an assortment of nails and screws and fencing staples.

A different type of tool box is a special case to hold power tools. Shown is a router case; the same style box can be made to hold a portable circular saw, or portable electric drill and accessories. A case not only keeps everything together and handy in the shop, but allows you to carry tools on the job without losing or damaging them or their accessories.

Nail Tray

Another handy shop accessory is the nail tray. It keeps nails sorted and handy for a variety of jobs and beats rummaging through a dozen or so paper sacks looking for just the right nail for the job. It can be made easily of scrap lumber.

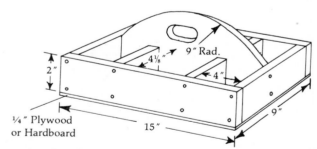

Another time-saver is the nail tray, made of lightweight scrap lumber.

Lumber Rack

If you plan to keep any materials in the shop, a good rack to hold lumber above ground, level and flat, is necessary. In a small shop, you can often use the joists of an open ceiling for the same purpose.

Chapter 2   Hand Tools

In today's high-speed style of living, if we need a board cut, we turn on a power saw and quickly and effortlessly cut it. Or, if we need a hole drilled, we push a power-driven bit through in seconds. Many of us have almost forgotten that there is another way of doing these jobs: using hand tools. Museums all over the world are filled with exquisite and beautiful furniture made many years ago, entirely by hand tools.

The convenience of today's "easy-does-it" power tools has made many craftsmen unaware of the capabilities and uses of the simple, time-tested hand tools.

Hand tools will never replace power tools, but then power tools will never replace hand tools. For instance, when building a cabin in the country or working on farm outbuildings, you may not have electricity available. Working on a boat while it is in the water is a hazardous thing to do, even with today's double-insulated power tools. So the object is to pick the best of both, using each tool for the purpose for which it is intended. There are also many craftsmen who derive extra pleasure from making something with the simplest of means, and hand tools are their answer.

Buying hand tools is the first step, and it's easy; buy tools as you need them. Good hand tools are not cheap, but they're well worth their price. If cared for and used

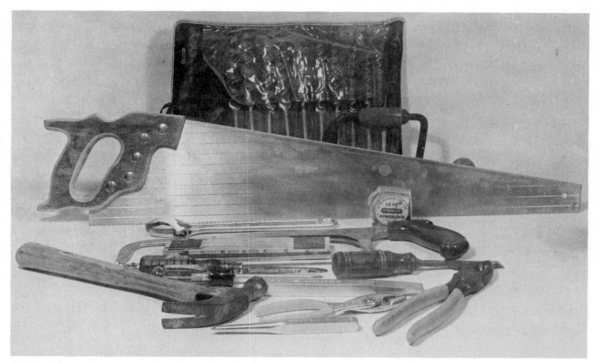

With these tools, you can handle most jobs, from installing a new screen to building a greenhouse.

properly, they will last your lifetime and maybe your children's. I inherited some of my best tools from my grandfather.

A good basic "starter" set of tools that can be used for almost any home maintenance job and for most building projects would include:

1. *Hammer.* A 16 ounce claw hammer would be a good choice.

2. *Handsaw.* A 26-inch handsaw with eight points to the inch is considered the best for general carpentry work. For finer work, choose one with 10 points to the inch.

3. *Folding wooden rule.* Buy a rule with an extension to enable you to measure inside openings such as doors or windows.

4. *Metal tape rule.* A 12-foot rule is usually long enough for most general work. Choose one with a lock to hold the tape in place.

5. *Combination square.* This handy device combines a miter square, depth gauge, marking gauge, rule and a "try square" for measuring squareness of planed and sawn edges.

6. *Chisel.* Buy only a wood chisel made of good steel. A chisel made of poor metal can't hold an edge and is dangerous. Chisels purchased in sets are more economical, but if you must buy only one chisel buy a ⅜-inch; you can then easily make mortises of ⅜- or ¾-inch and the chisel is still wide enough for most other work.

7. *Pliers.* A thin, straight-nose, combination, slip-joint plier is the best all around buy for a "one-plier" toolbox It can be used for almost any job from cutting to electrical work or as a wrench.

8. *Screwdriver.* Both a "flat-blade" and a "Phillips" are required. Again buy tools of good metal, or they'll bend out of shape or the end will break and pop off at the wrong moment.

9. *Push drill.* A good push drill purchased with a set of small drills can be used for almost any small drilling job around the house. It can easily and quickly be used for starting nail or screw holes.

10. *Brace and bits.* For larger holes you will need a brace and a set of bits. A full set of bits is expensive, but lasts a lifetime.

With this set of tools and a good tool box to store them, you should be able to handle almost any job around the house or farm. And, you can always add more tools as you need them.

Using tools properly is important not only to get the job done, but for safety reasons as well.

Hammers

A favorite saying among carpenters and craftsmen is "if it doesn't fit, get a bigger hammer and make it fit." There is a lot of truth in that old saying. A hammer is not just a hammer; there are all different kinds and each does a specific job better than others.

When you buy a hammer, buy the best. A good hammer, like most tools, will last a lifetime and can be handed down proudly from generation to generation. Another reason for buying the best is that a hammer is a very personal tool. After a couple of years of use, a favorite, well-used hammer begins to fit your hand like an old glove.

HAMMER SIZES. The choice for a hammer to be used for most general work would be a 16 oz. hammer with either a wooden handle or plastic or steel shank. The three handles dampen shock about equally well; the choice is merely a matter of opinion. The hammer must be a good name brand. A cheap one will shatter like a piece of glass if hit just right, and a piece of flying metal from the hammer face can be really dangerous.

If most of your work will be heavy, such as framing buildings or working around a farm or ranch, you might prefer a heavier hammer weighing up to 20 ounces. If you do a lot of indoor house finishing or cabinet or fine furniture work, you'll want a smaller finishing hammer. These weigh 12 to 16 ounces.

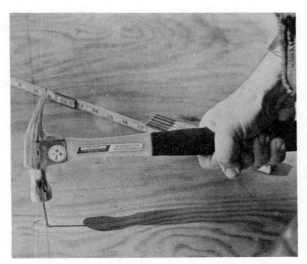

A 16 oz. hammer with fiberglass handle and neoprene grip used to drive flooring nails.

CORRECT USE. Learning to use a hammer correctly is an important aspect of good woodworking. If not used properly, a hammer will wear you out in a short time, but with a little practice and the right kind of swing you can hammer all day as do carpenters and cabinetmakers.

The secret is to allow the weight of the hammer to do most of the work. Don't try to force the hammer down any harder than its natural weight will let it fall; just guide it and keep your arm and shoulder loose. Don't pull the hammer up with a stiff elbow swing. Allow your arm to swing freely at the elbow. Grasp the hammer handle near the end, where it narrows down. Too many people "choke" a hammer handle, grasping too near the head, which creates a lot more work and doesn't allow the hammer to "fall" naturally.

15

When pulling nails, use a wood block under the hammer head to prevent marring and to gain more leverage.

HAMMER FACE. The face of your hammer is extremely important and you must keep it clean and in good shape. If you notice you're bending more nails than usual, look at the face; it may be scratched or covered with wood resin or glue. Place a piece of fine sandpaper down flat on your workbench and use it to polish the face. Don't, under any circumstances, grind the face of the hammer flat. The face is de-

Use sandpaper to clean a hammer face.

signed for striking the nail head evenly, and is rounded, enabling you to drive a nail-head flush with a wood surface without denting the wood.

When driving nails in fine finish work such as on a cabinet or trim, drive the nail to just above the surface of the wood, then use a nail set to drive the nail below the wood surface. The small hole left by a finishing nail can then be filled so it's almost unnoticeable.

BALL-PEEN HAMMER. The second most important hammer to the craftsman is a ball-peen hammer. This hammer

Peen hammers are good for fastening rivets.

should be used for metal working; save your woodworking hammer for driving nails only. Ball-peen hammers come in several sizes as well as styles, and keeping both a lightweight one (16 ounce) and a heavy weight (two pound) will be handy.

Probably the most common use of a ball-peen hammer is to drive punches and metal chisels, or just to pound metal when the need arises.

The rounded end of a ball-peen makes it a most versatile tool. It is often used to close metal rivets; a less-known use is in making engine gaskets. Merely lay the gasket material over the opening. Tap with the rounded end at the location of the bolt holes. The rounded end will push the gasket material into the bolt holes and you've got your gasket positioned and marked very easily. Don't allow the gasket material to be cut entirely through by the hammer or you may end up with pieces of gasket material in hard-to-get-at places.

If the ball of a ball-peen hammer is kept clean and polished it can be used to put a decorative "peened" surface on a metal object such as a brass or copper ash tray or candy bowl. For this operation, a metal "stake" or rounded metal ball clamped firmly in a vise is used as an anvil to support the work. The hammer is allowed to drop onto the metal work with a bounce to produce a good clean "dent." The dents must be placed randomly, but also must be approximately the same size to produce a good-looking piece of work.

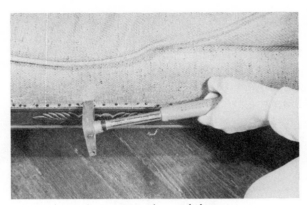
Furniture work is easy with a tack hammer.

TACK HAMMER. Another hammer that really comes in handy is a good tack hammer. Choose one with a magnetized end rather than one with a magnet slipped in a drilled hole in the end of the hammer. Those with the glued-in magnet invariably come apart after a little use. With practice, you'll learn to spread tacks out on a workbench, pick one up with the magnetized end of the hammer, tap it into place, reverse the handle head quickly and drive the tack home, all within seconds.

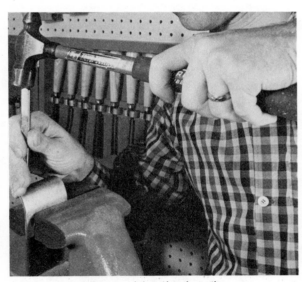
Ball-peens are also good for chisel work.

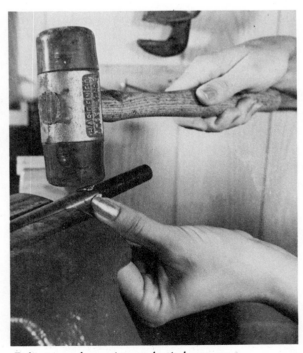
Delicate work requires a plastic hammer.

SLEDGE. For heavy-duty metal work, you'll want a sledge or blacksmith's hammer. These vary in weights from two to ten pounds and can be used for everything from pounding stakes to driving metal pieces together or apart.

17

MALLET. A workshop should also include either a wooden, rubber, or leather mallet, or a plastic-tipped hammer for delicate jobs that require gentle taps and no hammer marks. Anyone who does any refinishing work will appreciate these hammers. With a little light tapping, stubborn furniture parts can be driven apart or refitted without fear of damaging an antique finish.

These hammers are also well suited for fine work on soft metals such as brass, copper or silver.

SHINGLING HATCHET AND BRICK HAMMER. Two hammers which may not be found in the home craftsman's tool box are shingling hatchets and brick hammers. Both are builder's tools. A shingling hatchet is a small hatchet with a flat face on one side of the head for driving shingling nails. The hatchet can be used by an expert to cut shingles quickly to size and the hatchet head is used as a gauge to measure runs of shingles.

The brick or block hammer is used to split bricks or concrete blocks. An expert can split a brick in seconds, scoring each side with quick taps of the sharp hammer point, turning the brick until it breaks at the score line.

Hammers are very important tools to any craftsman, whether he is a woodworker, bricklayer or tinner, and choosing and using the correct hammer for the job is a big step toward good craftsmanship.

Handsaws

One of the homesteader's most important tools is the handsaw. If the primary aim is to complete simple home repairs, only one type of saw may be necessary. On the other hand, a dedicated wood craftsman may own as many as a half-dozen good handsaws, each suited for a particular job.

CROSSCUT SAW. The saw used most by the woodworker, and probably the one owned by the one-saw home-owner is a crosscut saw. Crosscut saws are used for cutting across the grain of the wood. A crosscut saw cuts on both the forward and backward strokes. Crosscut saws are available with relatively coarse teeth, or with many other grades including those that are extremely fine.

Saws are designated by the term, "points to the inch," or rather teeth to the inch. An extremely fine crosscut saw would have 10, 11 or even 12 points to the inch. The number of points or teeth to the inch gives the size of the teeth of the saw.

A shingling hatchet with gauge pin.

A hammer for brick and concrete.

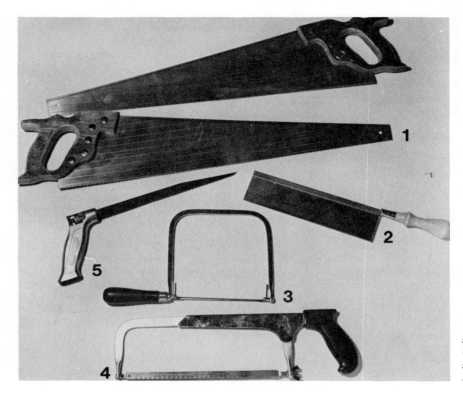

"Handsaws" come in many styles, and include wood saws (1), backed saws (2), coping saws (3), hacksaws (4) and key-hole saws (5).

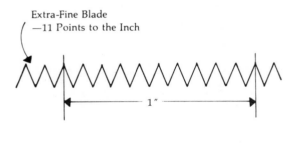

Extra-Fine Blade
—11 Points to the Inch

1″

Coarse Blade
—8 Points to the Inch

1″

Points per inch indicate saw coarseness.

A coarse, seven-point saw is about right for cutting in green or wet wood. An eight-point saw is used for most normal cross-cutting and cuts fast yet smoothly. For more exacting woodworking, a 10-point saw would be required. An 11- or 12-point saw might be desired for very exacting work. A fine-toothed saw will make an extremely fine cut, but it cuts slowly and should be used only on light, dry wood.

Handsaws are also designated by the length of the toothed portion of the blade and blades are 16 to 26 inches long. A 24- or 26-inch saw is used for most purposes. If used and cared for properly, a good crosscut saw will last a lifetime, and probably will be handed down to the next generation.

One of the main problems when using a crosscut saw is ensuring that its blade doesn't become bound or twisted. To ensure this, use two sawhorses or other devices to hold the board to be sawn in position. Always place the board to be cut with the cutting line outside the sawhorses. If the board is cut between the sawhorses it will bind on the saw and not only make it hard to continue sawing, but possibly damage the saw blade as well.

With the board properly positioned, mark the line to be cut. Use a square such

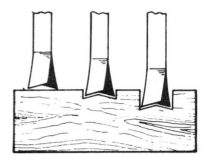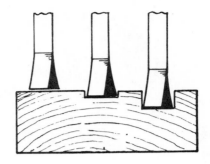

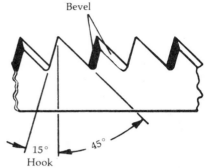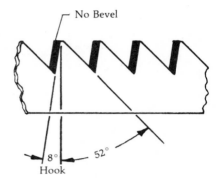

Bevel

No Bevel

15°
Hook

45°

8°
Hook

52°

Crosscut saw teeth (left) are filed on a bevel, while ripsaw teeth (right) are square across and hooked at a sharper angle.

as a combination or carpenter's square to make sure the line is straight and square with one side of the board (unless otherwise desired). Place the saw in position with the teeth resting outside, but against the penciled line. The saw should be positioned with the butt of the blade down near the line, and short pull strokes should be made to start the saw cut correctly. Use your thumb to guide the saw blade in a straight cut until the cut is started, then move it out of the way. Lift the saw after each pull stroke until the saw cut is properly started, then shift into a relaxed full stroke, both pushing and pulling. Don't try to force the saw; use relaxed easy strokes, and let the sharp teeth of the saw do the work for you. It's easier to maintain a good straight line this way. Don't saw with short strokes and only in the center of the saw; it will not only wear you out, you'll dull the teeth in that section and wear the saw unevenly. Use your forefinger on the saw handle to help guide the saw and add support.

The work should be held solidly by holding and kneeling on it. The craftsman should be positioned directly over the line,

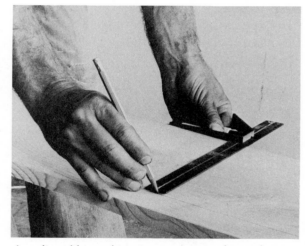

An adjustable combination square may be used to mark crosscuts or ripcuts.

so he can not only see the line easily, but tell if the saw blade is cutting straight and not being forced right or left. The toothed edge of the blade should be kept at about a 45-degree angle to the wood surface and strokes should be made with the entire arm. As you near the end of the cut, grasp the waste to prevent it from falling and tearing out a splinter. Make the last few strokes short and easy.

20

When sawing, keep a 45° blade angle.

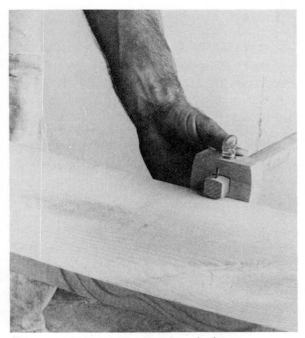

Gauge, set for marking along board edge.

RIPSAW. In most respects, a ripsaw is similar to the crosscut saw. One main difference is that the ripsaw cuts mostly on the forward stroke. The ripsaw is used for cutting with the grain. Usually a ripsaw has finer set teeth than a crosscut saw, but the cut is still a bit coarse. Ripsaws range from four to six points to the inch. All ripsaws are a standard 26 inches in length. The teeth on a ripsaw are square across rather than filed at an angle as on the crosscut saw.

The board to be cut with a ripsaw is placed lengthwise on the sawhorses. Mark the cutting line. There are two simple ways of marking a lengthwise line on a board. The first is to set a combination square so that it will slide along the edge of the board, the arm extended to just the amount to be cut. A pencil is positioned at the end of the arm and slid along with the square, marking the cutting line. The second and easiest method is to use a marking gauge. Merely set it for the width of the material to cut and slide along the edge of the board, marking the line as you go.

With the line marked, position the board at about knee high or on a good solid sawhorse. Position yourself directly over the line. Starting a cut with a ripsaw is exactly opposite from starting one with a crosscut saw. With a ripsaw, the blade should be positioned with the tip of the saw starting the cut. Start the cut using short little draw strokes until the saw kerf (cut) is well started and you're sure it's in the right spot. Then shift to long easy strokes and continue sawing. Remember not to force the saw; let it work for you.

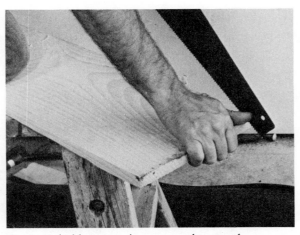

To start, hold saw as shown; use short strokes.

21

Cut on the outside (waste side) of the line. If you're sawing a long board, keep moving back with the cut and keep positioned comfortably for seeing the line and saw, and for operating the saw. If a long cut tends to close and bind on the saw blade, insert a wide wood chisel or wooden wedge in the end of the kerf to keep it open.

Whether a crosscut or ripsaw, it's important to take good care of it. An occasional wiping with light oil, both the blade and handle, is about all the maintenance required. Make sure you've got a specific place to store or hang the saw so it will be out of the way and protected from damage.

Backed saws come in all sizes from the tiny dovetail saws to huge 26-inch saws used in large miter boxes. Because of the thickness of the rigid backing along the saw back, these saws can only be used on materials that are not thicker than the width of the saw blade. Backed saws are sharpened in the same manner as crosscut saws, except the file must be smaller to fit into the tiny teeth.

Coping Saws

These saws with metal frames and tiny blades are used exclusively for cutting curved lines in wood. They're better used

Backed Saws

Backed saws are usually classified with crosscut saws. They're made in much the same way and used in much the same manner. However, there is less *tooth set* (angle of teeth to alternate sides) in backed saws and more points to the inch, producing extremely fine, but slow-cutting saws. These are particularly good for exacting work requiring either an extremely fine saw kerf or close tolerances in the cutting.

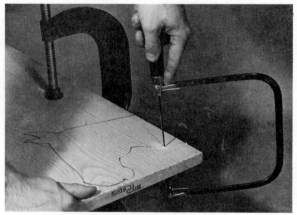

Coping saws are designed to cut curves.

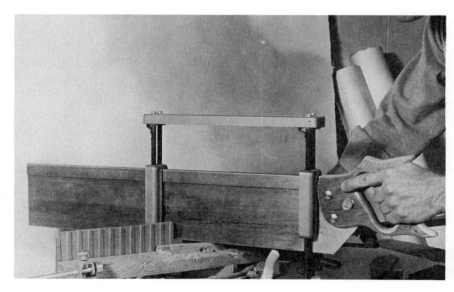

A backed saw, set in a miter box with stops for multiple blade angles.

22

on wood that is not too thick. A 2 x 4 takes a lot of cutting with a coping saw.

The blade may be removed and poked through a predrilled hole, then refastened to the saw and the saw used to cut inside circles, if the throat of the saw will clear the work. The blade may be positioned in any angle to the handle by moving little arms that position the blade. Both arms must be moved or the blade will twist and break.

Key-Hole Saws

Cutting access holes in paneling or wall boarding is a snap with these little saws. There's a variety of blades that will fit into the saws, for rough-woodcutting to fine-woodcutting and even metal cutting. These saws are also sometimes called general purpose saws because they may be used for cutting almost any materials.

The saw blades are disposable, and are thrown away rather than sharpened.

Hacksaws

Hacksaws are used for cutting metals, plastic, and even tile. They too use disposable blades; but buying cheap hacksaw blades is one good way of cheating yourself. They'll not only wear you out trying to

Before cutting, secure material firmly.

cut with them, but dull quickly and even break. Twice as many cheap blades as good blades are needed to do a job.

In using a hacksaw, the piece to be cut must be firmly held in a good solid vise, and it should be clamped so sawing is done as close to the vise as possible to prevent chattering. If sawing through thin, springy metal, two pieces of wood should be clamped, one on each side of the metal, and all sawed together. This prevents chatter and the possibility of bending or springing the metal out of shape.

Pliers

Pliers are one of the most basic, yet one of the most versatile tools. They come in almost more sizes and shapes than you can count. There are tiny electronic pliers that aren't much larger than tweezers; these delicate little instruments are used for grasping and holding fine wires and components together. On the other hand, there are pliers that weigh more than a pound used in heavy-duty mechanical work.

The one tool in almost every household is a pair of pliers. Unfortunately, many are made from cheap soft metal and they soon wear loose or break. Buying pliers is just like purchasing other tools: You usually get just what you pay for. Buy only name brand tools. If stored and used properly, these tools will last a lifetime, and, like most good tools, are a wise investment. Here are some of the pliers available:

UTILITY PLIERS. The most common plier is a slip-joint utility plier. These are found in almost every tool box and kitchen tool drawer. Usually, they are chrome-plated or highly polished and the two jaws may be adjusted to make a larger or smaller opening by turning the plier handles until the flat-sided bolt slips through the slot. These pliers come in all sizes and it's a good idea to have several.

Keep one in the house, one in your car, one in your tackle-box for replacing shear-pins and some in the shop.

SLIP-JOINT PLIERS. These pliers are also called *arc-joint pliers* and, if the jaws are smooth and not serated, they're called *water-pump pliers.* They are one of the most versatile tools to have and are excellent for several jobs. The jaws are slip-jointed so they can be adjusted to several different opening sizes. The jaws are also positioned so they are almost parallel in every open position. This makes them excellent for turning nuts or bolts. The larger sizes are used to remove stuck sink-trap fittings and other larger "nuts." Larger types with serated jaws can also be used for turning pipes in places that a pipe wrench can't reach.

Slip joint pliers help ease engine work.

LINEMEN'S PLIERS. These heavy-duty pliers have cutting edges on their sides and a serated nose used for grasping and twisting wires. The grips on these and all pliers intended for electrical work must be coated with a rubber or plastic material that is non-conductive and meets federal specifications. Linemen's pliers are an ex-

cellent choice for a second plier as they can be used for many jobs including wire cutting and heavy-duty bending.

STRIPPING PLIERS. Stripping pliers are an electrician's multi-purpose tool. They come in all different shapes, but their main purpose is stripping insulation from wires. Normally, they have places for stripping wire, sized 12 through 24 gauge.

Stripping pliers with protective grips.

Many of these pliers also have sharp edges for cutting wire, a crimper for installing crimp fittings on wire, and small serated jaws for bending and twisting wire. Naturally, the grips on these pliers are plastic coated for safety.

CUTTING PLIERS. There are many different configurations of cutting pliers, but the two most popular are diagonal or side cutters and end cutters or nail nippers. Side cutters come in many different sizes from tiny precision cutters used in electronic work to larger cutters used for cutting heavy-duty wire and small bolts. With their cutting edges on the front of the pliers they can cut materials off flush with a surface; and the position of the cutters close to the handles gives good leverage and helps when cutting harder and larger materials.

24

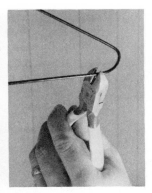

End cutters (left) and side cutters.

LONG-NOSE PLIERS. In the larger sizes, these pliers are called *chain pliers* and are equipped with side cutters as well as long serated jaws. These pliers are excellent for making wire loops and grasping objects in small tight places. In the smaller sizes, they are called *needle-nose,* and are essential in precision electronic work.

There are several unusual configurations of the jaws on these pliers. One shape is bent at right angles and makes easy work of reaching into corners of a chassis or circuit boards. Another shape has both jaws completely rounded with no flat serated edges. These pliers are excellent for grasping tiny hair-sized wire because they can't accidentally cut the fine wire with a flat edge. They are also great for making jewelry of precious metals as they can't nick or scar the metals during the bending process.

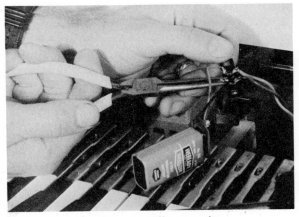

For precision work, use needle-nose pliers.

VISE-GRIP PLIERS. These are one of the handiest pliers a craftsman can own. The jaws on these pliers lock when they are squeezed shut around an object, making the pliers usable as an adjustable wrench, vise, or pipe wrench. The jaws on these pliers are serated and, on better models, a tripping lever allows them to be opened quickly. Turning a knob on the handle end adjusts the jaw opening to different sizes. These pliers are excellent for many jobs, including turning rusted nuts or bolts, or those with damaged heads that a regular wrench won't fit. They can also be used as "clamps" for holding small parts together to be glued, soldered, or even welded.

Vise grip pliers, tightened into position, are ideal for rusted or worn bolts.

UNUSUAL PLIERS. There are many different specialty pliers including: *snap-ring pliers* used for holding rings together while they are placed in position; *brake-shoe pliers* for easy removal of brake shoe springs; *fencing pliers* for nailing staples in place and twisting and cutting heavy wire; *hose-clamp pliers* for holding hose clamps; *hog-ringing pliers* used for fastening upholstery materials in place; and many others.

Every plier does its particular job the best. And good craftsmen know it's easier on their tools and themselves to use the tool designed for a particular job.

Keeping pliers in good working order requires little work. They should be sprayed occasionally with a good rust-preventive oil and wiped clean with a soft rag if used in moisture-laden areas, or if allowed to become damp or wet. Make sure plastic handles on electrician's pliers don't become nicked or cut; if damaged this way, they can cause a bad shock. If they become nicked, you can dip the handles in a rubber solution to recoat them.

Store your pliers in a rack that's easy to get to and keeps the pliers up off the workbench. Don't just throw them in a drawer with other tools; they'll soon become dirty, and maybe even damaged, or their hard-cutting edges may damage other tools.

Levels

One of the handiest tools a do-it-yourself homeowner can own is a good level. One will usually do almost any leveling job you might have around the home. A good all-purpose level is a high-quality, 24-inch aluminum level. With this size you can do almost any job, but the level is small enough to pack into a tool box or hang over a workbench.

A level has two or more vials so you can read the level in the horizontal position, or find plumb by reading the level in the vertical position. Some levels such as the smaller torpedo levels contain a 45-degree vial as well. Newer levels have easily changeable vials so you can remove a broken vial and replace it with a new one. Levels come in all sizes from tiny pocket levels to giant 78-inch levels with built-in extensions.

USING LEVELS. To use the level, place it in position and take a reading to determine "level" or plumb, depending on the position of the level. Either lift up on one end, or pull it out from the surface to determine how far off the surface is. The vial

bubble should float exactly in the center of the vial. When leveling a long surface, even a "smidgeon" off, with the bubble just barely showing under one line, can make a lot of difference.

A level may be used in either a vertical or horizontal position.

When using a level for mortar work always check to make sure there aren't any pieces of dried mortar sticking to the level that could distort the reading. This happens often when mortar is really "flying" and you're trying to lay a good number of concrete blocks.

DIFFERENT SIZES. When you have long objects to level, for instance, a mobile home, or a long kitchen cabinet, you can't beat a long, 78-inch level. This level gives accurate readings over long distances. One good rule is to use as long a level as will fit on the surface.

For leveling long surfaces, a 48-inch level is handy.

Some long levels have extensions, adding several feet to their length. Some are up to 10 feet long. And better levels of this type have extensions that lock in place. Others have magnetic edges that hold them in place on steel girders and metal door frames. A shop-made extender can be made with a 10-foot length of white pine or sugar pine 2 × 4. Make sure the lumber is well seasoned. It's a good idea to measure it with a shop caliper and allow it to set for about a week, then measure again to insure the material is stable.

A good level will last a lifetime. I inherited two levels, and, with a little care, they should remain usable for my son as well. One is an aluminum two-footer, the other a 48-inch wooden level. Long, high-quality wooden levels have their edges banded with metal to prevent damage to the wood or other damage which might throw the level off.

Aside from the traditional 24-, 48- and 78-inch levels, there are several other sizes, including 18-inch wooden levels and the nine-inch torpedo-shaped level. Most high-quality smaller levels are made of wood or extruded aluminum and are also used for those small, hard-to-get-to jobs such as installing a threshold.

A shop-made extender beneath short level.

Plane one edge of the stock perfectly smooth, then turn the lumber over and plane the opposite edge. Use a pair of calipers to ensure the two edges are perfectly parallel. Find the exact center end-to-end and mark for a hand hole. Then place your level over the hand hole. Cut the edges of the board to taper down, lightening it a bit in weight. Varnish or lacquer it to keep out moisture.

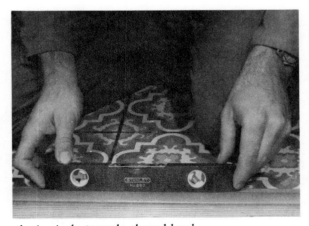

A nine-inch, torpedo-shaped level.

27

STRING LEVELS. One of the most uncommon levels, but one that pays for itself the first time around, is the string level. Basically, this is used in concrete block work, and other heavy construction. It is nothing more than a tiny level with one vial and hooks on top of it. In use, a string is strung between two supports. The string is pulled taut to ensure there is no sagging and the line or string level is hooked in place. A reading is taken and the string moved to make the vial level. This string can then be used as a guide to lay the blocks. The string level is also great for laying rock walls, starting foundations, and almost any other graded concrete work.

An angle finder or automatic protractor may be used to determine how perpendicular a wall is.

A string level is ideal for laying foundations and concrete walls.

Most good string levels have pocket clips so you can carry them around in your shirt pocket, as well as feet on their bottom edges to enable you to use them as miniature surface levels.

SPECIALIZED LEVELS. There are several other kinds of specialized levels, including tiny machinists' levels for determining true parallelism of surfaces, and bull's-eye levels that are circular and can be used to determine level in all horizontal directions. You've often seen these tiny

levels used on wheel balancers in an auto repair garage. You can purchase these levels for less than $1; and some have a peel-off sticky back so they can adhere to almost any object.

One of the newest types of levels is the automatic protractor, or level indicator. These are placed flat against a surface and a needle goes around a dial indicating the amount of angle the surface is from plumb or level. These are great for determining how perpendicular a wall is, when you wish to join another wall onto it. You could also use these new devices to lay out a patio. By using the protractor and a long wooden extender board you could determine the exact fall needed to insure good water runoff.

Whether you own one level or many, these are high-quality precision tools and they should be stored in a safe place so they won't get dropped, or treated roughly. The vials or level frame may be damaged easily. Don't store levels in hot spots, or leave them in the sun for any length of time or they may warp. If treated carefully, they'll give you a lifetime of service.

PLUMB BOBS. Most plumb bobs are heavy brass affairs that hang from strings

A plumb bob is used to determine and mark plumb lines for walls, doors, etc.

and have points on their bottom ends to indicate the exact plumb line. One of the easiest plumb bobs to use is a chalk line box shaped like a plumb bob. It can be suspended to indicate a plumb line, and, if against a solid surface, you can carefully hold the chalk line against the surface and snap it, giving a true plumb line for starting a new wall, or cutting a door or opening in an old wall.

Screwdrivers

Probably the most used and abused tool is the screwdriver. Almost everyone owns a screwdriver or two, and a woodworker usually owns a double handful. A screwdriver is a very versatile tool. It can, of course, be used for driving screws in wood, metal, plastic or whatever. It can also be used for prying off can lids, stirring paint, digging

out staples or bent over nails. A screwdriver could even be used for digging in the ground in an emergency.

I like to keep one good set of hardened metal screwdrivers for my fine furniture and such exacting metal work as gunsmithing. I then buy the cheap dime-store varieties by the dozen and use them for other chores. The cheap ones are made of soft metal and usually chip or wear, but they can also be easily reground to almost any shape and then eventually discarded.

BE CAREFUL. Never use an old and worn or chipped screwdriver when working with fine cabinet woods. The screwdriver blades won't fit the screw slot properly and can slip, causing a bad gouge in the wood. Worn screwdriver heads or screwdriver blades that are too small for the screw can also mar the screw.

If you're doing extremely exacting work, it's a good idea to grind the screwdriver blade to fit the screwhead slot.

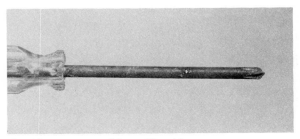

Avoid worn screwdrivers like this one.

Grind to proper angle, then "square" end.

29

Screwdrivers are tools not toys, and they should never be treated carelessly; one of the most dangerous uses of them is to use them as chisels. A screwdriver should never be pushed toward your face or body; a sudden slip and you've got a nasty gouge.

Screwdrivers should be treated with respect. Never allow children to play with these tools without adult supervision.

Screwdrivers used in electrical work should have good, non-conducting plastic handles. Wooden-handled screwdrivers will work, but they're sometimes dangerous because their metal ferrules come up high on the handle.

Always use the proper size and shape screwdriver for the job. Use as large a screwdriver as you possibly can. It will not only prevent the blade from slipping from the screw slot, but will provide you with more leverage.

The easier it is to drive the screw, the less chance of a slip with the screwdriver and the resulting gash to the wood surface, or yourself. Always pre-drill holes for screws, even in soft woods. Even if you're able to drive the screw without the holes, you run the chance of splitting the wood around the screw. For a good fit, it is necessary that the screw hole match the thickness of the screw shank, less the threads. If the hole is large enough that the screw will fall in it easily, the screw will be holding only by its point. Also, the screw hole should never be drilled more than two-thirds the length of the screw. It's a good idea when drilling a number of screw holes of the same size to wrap a piece of masking tape around the drill bit to mark the correct depth.

SPECIAL TECHNIQUES. Many woodworkers like to use a drill bit called a "screw sink." This bit is shaped like a screw with the lower end smaller than the top and with a large cutting head that cuts a hole for the screwhead to fit down in. Using this bit in a drill, a woodworker can fit the screw head flush with the wood surface

Predrill screw holes with special "bits."

or lower it beneath the surface to be filled with wooden plugs or wood putty.

Before turning in the screw, rub it across a block of beeswax. This will make it easier to turn in as well as to remove. Many old-timers used to drill a small hole in the end of their wooden-handled hammer and fill this with beeswax. The screw point could be pushed in the hole to cover it quickly with the lubricating wax.

If a screw starts to squeak and becomes extremely hard to turn in hardwood, remove it and rebore the hole slightly. If you don't, you may break the screw in the hole.

STANDARD AND SPECIAL SCREWDRIVERS. There are a great number of unusual-head screwdrivers used in manufacturing various items, but those used most often by the homeowner-woodworker are a standard bit, Phillips bit and reed-prince bit. There are hundreds of different kinds of screwdrivers, each for a specific job. The *automatic screwdriver,* one of the more unusual ones, has a blade that turns as the screwdriver handle is

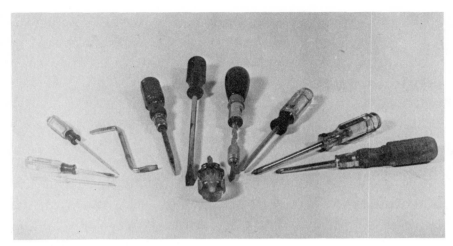

Screwdrivers come in many different sizes and shapes.

pushed down. As downward pressure is relaxed, a spring-loaded plunger helps return the screwdriver to an extended, "up" position. This tool is great for driving great numbers of screws as in boat building or cabinetwork. I worked for a cabinet shop for about five years, but I never quite mastered the art of driving door hinge screws quickly and efficiently with this tool.

A handy screwdriver for the mechanic is a small *offset screwdriver.* It is great for hard-to-reach spots.

Some other unusual screwdrivers include wedge-like, screw-holding drivers. These are great for reaching into tight spaces with a screw firmly held in position on the end of the screwdriver. There are also screwdrivers with ratchet handles for applying leverage to hard-to-turn screws.

STUCK SCREWS. If you're having trouble removing a stuck screw, the first step is to tap on the screwdriver handle lightly, while turning the handle. This may jar the screw enough to loosen it. If the screw is in metal and badly rusted, spray it first with a bit of WD-40 (a metal-protecting lubricant), give it about five minutes to work, then remove it.

If the screw starts but is extremely hard to turn, place a pair of vise grip pliers, or an adjustable wrench on the square shaft, not on the handle, to give yourself more leverage.

MAINTENANCE. Good screwdrivers, like any other good tool, should be properly maintained. Occasionally wipe with a good rust-proofing oil. Keep them hung up above your bench in a rack, or in the protective packages they come in. It's a good idea to have several different screwdriver sets. Keep one in a kitchen drawer for household tasks, some in your car for emergency repairs, and some in your shop.

Planes

Look in an old-timer's tool box, and you'll find several hand planes. Today much of the work formerly done with planes is done by power tools, but two of the most valuable tools, and handiest you may own, are a good jack plane and block plane.

Hand planes can be used for many jobs that are just about impossible with power tools. For instance, a dragging door may be quickly corrected by planing a bit of material off the dragging corner. Or a piece of wooden paneling may not quite fit in the area you measured it for. A few strokes on the edge with a good plane and the paneling will slide in and fit with that "grown-in-place" look.

There are basically two kinds of planes,

31

wooden and metal. Both are popular, and each has its followers. Metal planes are easier to adjust. The cutter on wooden planes is held in place by a hardwood wedge, and, to remove or adjust the cutter, you tap on the block to loosen the wedge.

The cutter on a metal plane, held in place by a series of screws and devices, may be adjusted laterally, forward or back, and up and down.

PLANE NOMENCLATURE (COURTESY STANLEY TOOL WORKS)

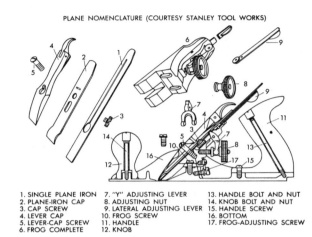

1. SINGLE PLANE IRON	7. "Y" ADJUSTING LEVER	13. HANDLE BOLT AND NUT
2. PLANE-IRON CAP	8. ADJUSTING NUT	14. KNOB BOLT AND NUT
3. CAP SCREW	9. LATERAL ADJUSTING LEVER	15. HANDLE SCREW
4. LEVER CAP	10. FROG SCREW	16. BOTTOM
5. LEVER-CAP SCREW	11. HANDLE	17. FROG-ADJUSTING SCREW
6. FROG COMPLETE	12. KNOB	

ADJUSTING PLANES. To many beginning woodworkers, plane adjustment and maintenance seem mystifying and complicated. They're not! On a metal plane, to remove the cutter blade for sharpening, or to loosen it for adjustment, merely lift the lifting lever and slide the lever cap off the screw. Lift the two-piece cutter out over the holding screw. To remove the cutter from the curling iron, turn the large slotted screw with a large screw driver holding the cutter in a vise. Many old-timers turn this screw with the wedged end of the lever cap, but if the screw is extremely tight you may mar the soft metal of the lever cap.

Turn the cutter blade 90 degrees to the curling iron and slide and lift it off the screw. Unless the cutter is extremely damaged such as might happen if you hit a nail (heaven forbid), the edge will need only honing on a good sharpening stone. It is

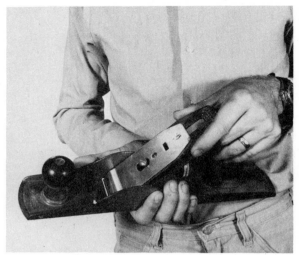

To remove plane cutter, first lift locking lever, then two-piece cutter.

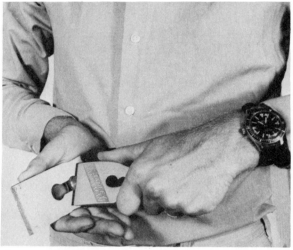

On most planes, the cutter may be separated, using the end of the lifting lever cap to unscrew the slotted screw.

very important to maintain the proper angle of the edge. In most cases this is 25 degrees. There are several good devices on the market that will hold the plane cutting edge in place on the hone, maintaining the proper edge angle.

To adjust a plane cutter sideways, or laterally, lift the lifting lever to loosen the cutter, then push the lateral adjust lever right or left to move the cutter edge right or left. The cutter edge should be straight and true with the sole of the plane.

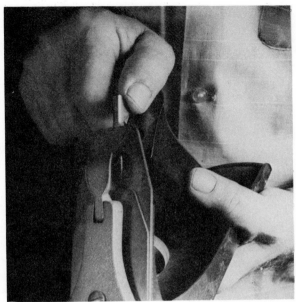

Move lateral adjustment lever to ensure the cutting edge is straight.

The depth of cut may be adjusted by turning the depth of cut adjustment screw on the back of the plane frog. This may be adjusted without loosening the lifting lever on most planes. The cutter depth should be set so that the plane cuts off a smooth thin curl of wood without gouging or digging in. Make a trial pass; then adjust the cutter depth until you achieve the correct shaving. Always cut with the grain of the wood. Cutting against the grain will cause the plane cutter to dig out tiny wood chips and gouge the wood surface.

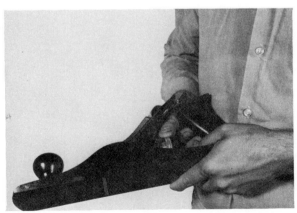

Turn depth adjustment screw as shown to ensure proper plane cutting depth.

The frog on metal planes may also be adjusted backwards or forwards by loosening the two frog screws, then turning the frog adjusting screw. This opens or closes the mouth of the plane. For most general purpose work and rough cutting, the mouth should be fairly open. For finer work, or for wood that tears easily, close the mouth up a bit.

If shavings fill up the mouth, the first adjustment to make is to adjust the depth to make a somewhat shallower cut. Loosen the blade, remove the jammed wood shavings, and make another trial cut. If the wood shavings still jam the mouth, it is too small and should be opened.

USING PLANES. Using a plane properly takes practice, but with a little experience a woodworker can use a plane skillfully, leaving glass-smooth wood surfaces that require little or no sandpapering. Here are four good rules to follow:

1. *Make sure the blade is sharp and true.* Like most woodworking tools, a dull blade not only won't cut properly, it is down right dangerous and causes the woodworker to push harder and harder, resulting in a slip or even bad fall.

2. *Make sure the work to be planed is securely and properly clamped.* For most work a good solid woodworking vise is the answer.

3. *Take a good easy, legs-spread-wide-for-balance stance.* You should be able to take a long easy planing stroke without moving your feet.

4. *Have a good firm, but relaxed grip on the plane and keep the plane flat and true on the work surface.*

One mistake made by some beginning woodworkers is rounding the corners of a planed edge. This comes from applying too much pressure at the start and end of the stroke. Try to keep the pressure even through the stroke.

Always plane across grain first if you're

planing all four edges of a piece of stock. Then turn the stock and plane with the grain. This will remove any splintering caused by planing across grain first. Another solution to this problem is to clamp small blocks to prevent splitting at the cross grain strokes.

The two most important planes to the average home-shop woodworker are a *jack plane* and a *block plane.*

JACK PLANE. This medium-sized plane, about 14 inches long, is literally the jack-of-all planes. It can be used for almost any job from trueing up a wood surface to planing a door, or even beveling the edge of a surface. It's the plane for a "one-plane" woodworker.

BLOCK PLANE. The second most popular plane, and the one I consider the handiest, is the block plane. This tiny plane is about four to five inches long and can be kept in a carry-about tool box easily. It can be used for almost any job from cutting down a piece of paneling to putting the final smoothing touches on a table top edge. Its small size makes it a favorite with cabinetmakers and, if the edge is pitched at a low angle, it makes a great "jointer" for edging plastic laminate. It is also great for making edge grain cuts, as

Block plane, ideal for finish work.

well as those delicate final adjustment cuts that make two pieces of wood look like they "grew together."

Two other planes often found in a woodworkers tool box are the *jointer* and *smoothing plane.*

JOINTER PLANE. This plane, usually about 22 inches long, is ideal for cutting down wood surfaces smoothly and precisely. Its long length enables the plane to ride over bumps and hollows; this feature makes the plane easy to use and produces fine results.

The mid-sized, all-purpose jack plane.

Twenty-two inch long jointer plane.

34

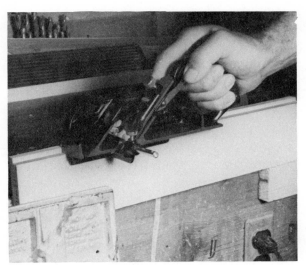
This plane cuts "rabbets" on stock edges.

SMOOTHING PLANE. This is a short plane used for glass-like smooth surfaces. It is kept adjusted to produce an extremely thin and fine shaving.

There are many other specialty planes that can be used for specific jobs; they include:

1. *Router planes*—for cutting dadoes and such things as routing out stringers for stair steps.

2. *Plough planes*—primarily for cutting dadoes.

3. *Rabbet planes*—for cutting rabbets (grooves) on edge of stock.

4. *Forty-five planes*—for cutting an edge to a 45-degree angle.

5. *Tongue-and-groove planes*—for cutting tongue-and-groove joints on edge of stock.

6. *Bullnose plane*—cutter edge is at front of plane for planing into corners.

7. *Compass plane*—for planing rounded surfaces.

MAINTENANCE. Planes are fine precision tools that will last a lifetime if cared for properly. They should never be stored sitting flat on the workbench or in a drawer. The cutting edges will dull quickly and easily in this manner. Instead, place small ¼-inch blocks under the front edge of each plane and keep the cutting edge just off the surface.

Wooden planes should be wiped down occasionally with a light coating of linseed oil. Metal planes should be sprayed with a light coat of penetrating, rust-proof oil, then wiped with a clean rag.

Chisels and Gouges

Skill with hand tools, especially chisels, is the mark of a fine craftsman. When it comes to trimming out a house, or building a beautiful piece of intricate furniture, the craftsman who is skilled with chisels really shines.

Chisels are extremely important tools for any craftsman's tool box, and most craftsmen have a variety of sizes and shapes. I'm including gouges with wood chisels because they're used not only for woodcarving but for many woodworking jobs such as carving recessed chair seats. Gouges come in all different sizes and shapes from round to v- or thin line-cutters called "veiners," and are used to cut material in a "scoop" fashion. One of the most important gouges is the "bent gouge," used to reach into deep areas and "scoop" out material. To keep gouges sharp, use a rounded sharpening stone made especially for honing rounded blades.

GET THE BEST. Like most hand tools, you should have the best in chisels. Not only will they last a lifetime, but they're easier to sharpen and much safer and easier to use. Good chisels are made of high-carbon steel and take an edge like a razor. It is not unusual to see an old-time craftsman with chisels you can shave with. Cheap chisels are made of soft steel and their sharpened edges will fold over like butter the first time they touch wood. Dull

Gouges can be used for making recessed seat bottoms for rocking chairs.

chisels are hard to use and can slip and cause dangerous accidents.

Good chisels are made of one piece of steel, with a center core running from the tang through a molded hard-plastic handle and connected to a metal end cap which provides a good striking surface. (Some very fine wood chisels have pointed tangs driven into wooden handles, but these chisels are made for hand use only, and should never be struck with a hammer.)

UPKEEP AND STORAGE. A good chisel requires little upkeep, but it should be honed frequently to keep the edge razor sharp, and it should be wiped occasionally with a good rust-preventive oil.

Chisels should never be stored loose in a drawer. They collect rust easily when enclosed and, after banging and rolling against each other, they become dulled and chipped. Instead, keep your chisels in an easy-to-get-to holder on the back of your workbench. If the holder allows the chisel edges to touch the workbench as mine does, place a thin sheet of cork (available at sporting goods stores for covering inside of tackle boxes) under the chisel edges.

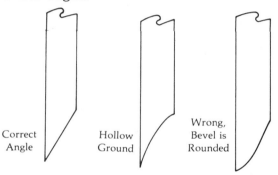

Correct Angle   Hollow Ground   Wrong, Bevel is Rounded

Keep chisel blade angles straight or slightly hollow ground. Never round blade edge.

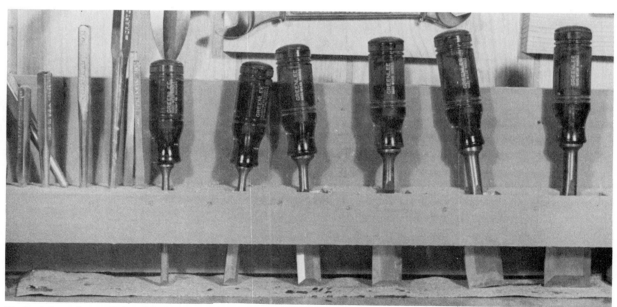

Cork strip at base of chisel holder prevents dulling of edges.

In case a chisel edge does become badly nicked, it will have to be reground. The edge should be ground to exactly the existing angle or somewhat "scooped" or hollow ground. A chisel edge should never be ground to a rounded shape. This causes the chisel to bounce back when struck, rather than dig in for a sharp, smooth cut.

USING CHISELS. There are two ways to use chisels: They may be used by pushing with the heel of one hand and guiding with the finger of the other, or by holding with one hand and striking with a hammer. The first method is used when there's little material to be removed and a good smooth cut is needed. With this method, a skilled craftsman can remove a beveled edge, or cut a shallow mortise that looks like it was "molded" in place, without sanding or extra smoothing. The second method, using a hammer, is for making deep "stop-cuts" or "marking" cuts, or for removing large chunks of material. Either the front or back of the chisel may be used depending on the job to be done.

When making stop cuts or marking cuts, the flat edge of the chisel is held against the line and the chisel held upright and tapped with the hammer. To remove material from between these lines, the chisel is turned over and the angle edge placed down. By tapping or pushing, chips are cut and forced out, yet the chisel will keep trying to ride up out of the cut rather than pull itself deeper. This method is used to make a nice, neat bottom in a mortise or cut.

When possible, chisel cuts should be made with the grain. When used in this manner, the chisel will also try to ride back out as the grain forces the chisel edge up. Cutting against the grain will cause the chisel to work deeper than you may wish. Cutting across the grain should be avoided wherever possible as this tears the wood away leaving uneven areas and splinters.

BE CAREFUL. Chisels are sharp and dangerous tools when misused. Never, in any circumstances, pull or strike the chisel toward any part of your body. One common mistake is to pull the chisel upward toward yourself. One day as a youngster I sneaked into my father's shop to play with his tools. I placed a piece of wood in a vise and proceeded to pull the chisel up with both hands towards my face. The chisel slipped in my unskilled hands and I received a bad cut under the end of my nose that required some stitches. I was lucky! Others have lost an eye doing what I did.

Another dangerous practice is to hold the work with one hand and push the chisel toward the holding hand. Again, a simple slip can mean not only a bad cut, but maybe the loss of a finger. Chisels are not toys and children should not be allowed to use them unless supervised carefully by an adult. Again, whether a child or an adult is using the chisel, it should be as sharp as possible. A sharp tool is easier to control and cuts without undue pressure. A dull tool will dig in, then pop out causing serious injury.

Chisels are extremely valuable tools to

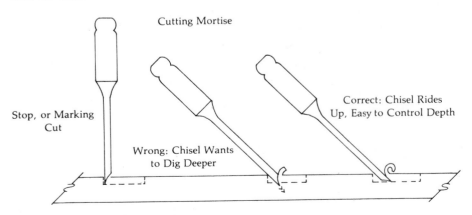

Cutting Mortise

Stop, or Marking Cut

Wrong: Chisel Wants to Dig Deeper

Correct: Chisel Rides Up, Easy to Control Depth

To make stop cuts, use chisel's flat side; to remove chips, place angled edge down.

any craftsman and learning to use them skillfully is both easy and essential.

Boring Tools

Almost every craftsman today owns an electric drill, but only a few old-timers own a full set of braces and bits, hand drills and all the accessories. But these old-time tools can still do many jobs today that modern high-speed drills can't do as well. Hand drills can be used anywhere, without electricity. If you're working on a boat, building a cabin back in the woods, or putting a gate on a fence, just pack along a brace and a set of bits.

BRACE AND BITS. The most popular hand boring tools are the brace and bits. Braces come in all different sizes and shapes for specific jobs, but the most popular is a medium brace with a 10-inch sweep. These give you enough leverage for even the hardest of woods, yet allow you to work in most places. The better braces have a ratchet that releases and re-

verses allowing you to turn the center handle freely in any direction without affecting the bit. This is great for working in corners and other confined places where you can't make a full circle with the handle.

To accompany this fine-quality tool you need a good set of auger bits. These come in sizes from ¼ to 1 inch and are usually sold in sets. Make sure you get a good, high-quality carbon steel set of bits or you'll never keep them sharp enough to work with. A woodworker can invest almost $40 in this combination of tools, but, if versatility is desired, it's worth it.

To use the brace and bit, the workpiece must be firmly clamped in position, allowing the woodworker to drill either horizontally or vertically. The main objective is to ensure that the bit is perfectly square with the workpiece so that the holes bored will be square. If you're boring down, it's a good idea to place your chin on your hand. This not only gives more pressure, but helps keep the bit aligned properly. After boring through the workpiece, turn the brace handle in reverse, gently pulling the bit out of the bored hole.

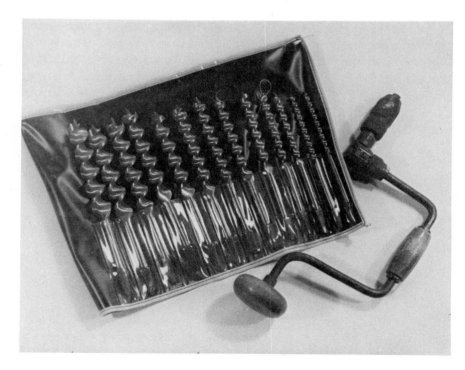

A brace with a good set of bits is a worthwhile investment.

38

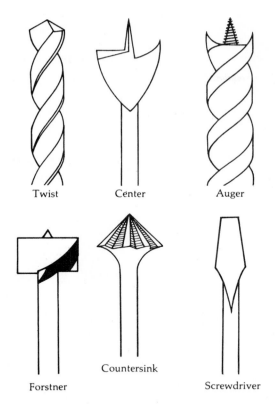

Twist Center Auger

Forstner Countersink Screwdriver

Some common bits.

To make large holes in thick woods, use an expansion bit with adjustable blade.

OTHER BITS. Other bits used in the brace include the center, forstner, expansion, countersink and screwdriver bits.

The center bit is also called a *"spade" bit* and is often used in electric drills. It is used primarily for boring through thin pieces of wood such as paneling. Regardless of the type of bit used, if you wish the back of the hole to be smooth and not splintered, back it up with a piece of waste wood before you bore.

One of the most versatile bits is the *expansion bit*. It comes with an adjustable sweep blade that allows you to bore a hole of any size up to the limits of the cutter blade (normally three inches). These bits are particularly useful for boring holes for door locks, and for drilling holes for bird house openings. There's one disadvantage to using expansion bits for boring in thin woods: Once the screw point penetrates through the wood it no longer pulls the bit with it and then considerable force must be used to finish the hole, which some-

times causes it to splinter. To prevent splintering, back the hole with waste wood scrap.

One of the best bits for fine furniture makers is the *forstner bit.* This bit is shaped with a circular cutting edge that protrudes almost as much as the point of the bit and is for making extremely precise holes in hardwoods. It is especially useful for making stopped holes, as the center point doesn't project a great deal.

For cutting a depression for screw heads you can use a *countersink bit,* after the screw hole has been drilled. It comes with a combination shank to fit either a brace or electric drill.

One unusual bit is a *screwdriver bit.* This comes in several different sizes and, when used with a brace, can provide the pressure and leverage to drive large screws in hardwoods.

HAND DRILL. Another type of drill is the hand drill. These are used with the smaller twist-type of drill bits for drilling holes ¼ inch or smaller. They are held by a top handle and operated by turning a crank. A drill with a double-gear drive is better than one with a single gear because it makes turning the handle much easier.

When using these drills, it's a good idea to pre-start the hole using a good awl, center punch or nail.

This type of drill is difficult to hold

Prestart holes for the hand drill bits with an awl, center punch or nail.

various sizes are stored in the handle of the drill.

Drills, braces and bits are all fine-quality tools which should keep a lifetime if cared for properly. Make sure you keep the bits in their protective pouch rolled up and stored in a safe place. Keep drill bits stored separately so they won't dull their cutting edges. Occasionally, spray the tools lightly with a good rust-preventive oil and wipe down the wooden handles with a bit of linseed oil.

straight while you crank. It is quite easy to wobble the drill around while turning the crank, which may cause the bit to break, or the hole to become too large.

Remove the drill bit frequently to keep it from becoming clogged with material.

PUSH DRILL. Another good hand tool is the push drill, which bores tiny holes and is ideally suited for precision work. It's also suitable for drilling nail holes used to assemble hardwood kitchen cabinets or for odd jobs such as drilling nail holes for hanging picture frames. Extra drill bits of

Sets of open-end and box-end wrenches.

Wrenches

A homesteader is by choice a jack of all trades; and with tractors, garden implements, and all their accessories, a good set of mechanic's tools is a must. A good choice includes: a ⅜-inch socket set, ½-inch socket set, a pair of adjustable wrenches (6 and 12 inches), a set of open-end wrenches and a set of box-end wrenches. One problem with farm machinery is the bolts or nuts often are bigger than most auto bolts or nuts, so you'll probably have to purchase larger tools for some repairs.

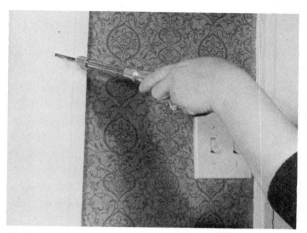

Push drill.

Measuring Tools

For most home and garden needs a simple 12-foot steel tape will do the job. Again, buy only the best. Not only will it last longer, it's easier to use and nothing is more frustrating than to have a tape that won't rewind properly. Incidentally, if you do happen to get one like that you can cut the tape into pieces and tack it down in places where you might make quick measurements such on on the side of a radial arm saw.

If you're planning on constructing many buildings, a 100-foot tape will save a lot of headaches and problems. However, they are costly and you might be able to borrow one. You may need a folding wooden rule.

A 100-foot, heavy-duty contractor's tape.

When you buy one make sure it has readings from 1-inch outward on both ends. Otherwise you may have it turned around and have to open it entirely to get to the starting point.

There are many other measuring tools; however, most are fairly specialized such as calipers for measuring metal thicknesses.

Files

You may need a good assortment of files for work around the home and shop. A good, flat, mill bastard file is probably the most valuable. It can be used for sharpening an axe in the field, for dressing down metal and a number of other things. In addition, you will also need specialized files for sharpening chain saws, and triangular files for sharpening saw blades. Purchase those only as you need them, and make sure they're the right size for your particular need.

Metal-Working Chisels and Punches

You may also need a variety of cold chisels and punches for working with rivets and other metal work around the garden and farm. Again, buy only good-quality, name-brand tools. Anytime you are using these tools wear safety glasses and hit chisels and punches only with a ball-peen or other metal-working hammer. The hardened face of a woodworking hammer will chip off easily and can cause a bad injury.

Hand tools may be used to teach children the fun of working with wood. Give a child a block of soft wood, a can full of No. 4 flat-head nails and a hammer. He'll do the rest! When he gets a little older, teach him how to use a saw. But don't give him a dull one; he'll try too hard with it, and possibly injure himself. When he has mastered the art of making that saw blade go where he wants it to, teach him how to measure and mark off what he wants to cut. Then give him plenty of small scraps and let him go to work.

He'll be building birdhouses, block cars and trucks, and things you never thought of. After he has learned how to correctly measure and carefully cut a board follow-

Children can learn to respect hand tools and use them with care.

ing a straight line with a saw, then plane the edges with a small plane and sand it thoroughly, he'll have no trouble learning to make a good square cut on a table or radial arm saw. And you'll breathe easier, knowing the respect he learns from hand tools, as a result of a few bumps and scratches, will remain when he later operates power tools.

Take good care of your hand tools; keep the cutting edges sharp and you'll be able to use them with ease and skill. Keep your tools stored on walls within easy reach, or in a good tool box stored off the floor. An occasional spray of WD-40 or similar penetrating oil and then a wiping with a soft cloth will keep them in perfect working condition for as long as you wish.

Wooden parts of your tools, or wooden tools also need care. About once a year wipe them off with a rag and a bit of linseed oil.

Get a good oil stone or sharpening stone. Buy a stone with one rough face and one smooth face. Keep the stone clean and learn to sharpen each tool properly. (See Chapter 4 on sharpening.)

Chapter 3

Power Tools

Power tools are not a necessity for most home and garden workshops. After all, our ancestors carved out their homes with nothing more than an axe and a sharp knife. On the other hand, some power tools can not only save time, they can make a job easy and pleasant.

Portable Electric Circular Saw

Probably the single most important power tool a small farm owner can have is a portable circular saw. These can be used for building fences, outbuildings and other things around the homestead as long as there is electricity near the site. Or for some buildings you may wish to precut the pieces and carry them to the building site.

DOUBLE INSULATION. When purchasing a portable electric circular saw or any power tool, make sure it's double insulated. Most new quality tools are double insulated. This is extremely important when using a power tool on a long extension cord, say out in a barn lot, chicken yard or garden, where you might be working on damp ground. Make sure the extension cord is grounded or plugged into a grounded circuit and that the third or grounding prong is left on and hasn't been broken off.

43

A portable electric circular saw.

from 6½-inch to 7¼-inch. Anything smaller won't cut through a 2 x 4 when set on a bevel. As a blade is sharpened it becomes smaller. And a blade that is completely buried in the cut causes the saw to run harder, so the best bet in most cases would be a 7¼-inch saw. When purchasing, check to make sure the base wraps completely around the blade. This is extremely important when cutting large sheets of plywood.

BLADES. Depending on the job to be done there are a number of blades that can be used in the saw:

1. *Combination/ripping blade*—for cutting with the grain of the wood.

2. *Chisel tooth combination blade*—for general ripping and cross cutting.

3. *Cross-cut blade*—for cutting across the grain of the wood.

4. *Plywood*—for fine finish cuts in plywood.

5. *Thin-rim plywood (hollow ground)*—for extra fine cuts on plywood, or fine end-grain cuts.

6. *Cross-cut flooring*—made of a special hard steel and used when cutting up used lumber that might have nails in it; it will withstand accidental nail contact better than most blades.

7. *Carbide tipped*—for cutting problem materials such as Masonite, Formica, asbestos and particle board.

8. *Metal-cutting blade*—for light metals.

9. *Masonry blade*—for concrete, brick, etc.

Double-insulated tools are just that: They consist of two different insulations. Both would have to fail for you to receive a shock. These tools have a plastic outside case or just the handle may be plastic, and normally they have a two-prong plug instead of a three-prong plug.

SUPPORT. To use a circular saw properly and safely, you must have something to support the work on, and in most cases the best bet is a pair of sawhorses. These should be sturdy, and high enough so you can work on them safely and without undue discomfort. As with all tools, follow safety rules when using a portable circular saw. First of all, read the recommendations in the owner's manual for safe operation of your saw.

There are several things to consider when purchasing a saw. A lot of farm and home work will be rough cutting thick lumber, such as 2 x 4s for studs. Most home craftsmen's saws have a blade size

PLYWOOD. Probably the single most important job of a circular saw is cutting large sheets of plywood. Even woodworking shops often have to make initial cuts in plywood with a portable circular saw, cutting the large sheet into smaller, easier-to-handle pieces. The main rule when cutting large sheets of plywood is to keep the plywood well supported. Pay special attention to the back or cut portion of the saw line. Otherwise, the plywood will sag and tighten on the saw blade, causing it to bind and eventually kick back or, even worse, jump completely out of the saw cut.

One solution is to place the plywood with the cut running lengthwise across two sawhorses. Make the cut until you get to the first saw horse, then move the plywood back or forward to prevent cutting the sawhorse. A better method is to place a couple of waste strips of wood across the top of the sawhorses, then adjust the saw blade so it just barely cuts through the plywood. You can then make the cut in one pass without having to move the plywood sheet. Above all, don't allow the cut or waste portion of the plywood to drop off as you finish the cut. Not only will this cause the saw to kickback, but it will probably cause the underside of the sheet to tear out as well.

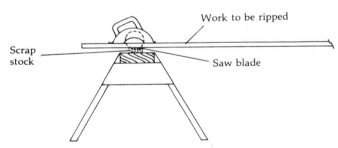

To protect sawhorse, use scrap wood when ripping or cutting board in two.

Marking a straight line across the plywood can be a problem. The best method is to measure and mark the desired location at both ends of the line. Then snap a chalkline stretched between these two points to establish a cutting line.

Another method of cutting along a line is to clamp a guide strip in place and allow the saw base to ride against the guide. Or, if the cut is near an edge, you can use the edge guide that is available as an accessory to the saw.

When cutting most materials, especially plywood, cut with the good side down because the blade cuts up through the material and it has less of a tendency to splinter the material in this position.

SAFETY. One of the most important safety rules when working outside on uneven ground is to make sure you have a good stable stance and won't stumble or fall over something on the ground while operating the saw. You should also make sure there is nothing on the ground that can catch the saw blade when you set it down, and make absolutely sure the blade has stopped running before you set it on the ground.

CROSS-CUTTING. Cross-cutting stock is fairly easy with a circular saw. Position the stock (if possible) with the largest part lying lengthwise across the sawhorse or horses and with the smaller (waste) part protruding out over the edge. Position yourself to the left hand side and make the cut with your right hand (reverse if left-handed), cutting so the saw blade cuts just to the right edge of the marked pencil line.

If you make the cut on stock such as a 2 x 4 or 1 x 12 with a smooth, even stroke, you won't have to support the work as you cut if off. Merely allow it to drop. However, if the stock protruding is very heavy and springy, it will drop down and bind on the saw blade, causing a dangerous kickback. You will have to support the waste end to prevent this. Always make sure the saw blade is clear of the stock before you turn the saw on, then carefully push the blade, revolving at full speed, into the work.

When setting the saw depth, set it to clear the thickness of the work, then increase it about ⅛ of an inch. If cutting small pieces, clamp them in place on the sawhorse. Never reach around and under the work being cut to hold it up. One of the most important rules is to use a saw blade that is sharp and has a good tooth set to it.

Most better saws will have bevel scales which allow you to make angled cuts. When making a bevel cut, the saw will normally operate best if it is pushed against a guide strip.

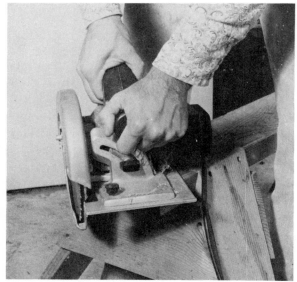
Saw can be adjusted for cutting depth.

Saw may be tilted to cut at an angle.

PLUNGE CUTTING. If you wish to cut out a piece from the center of a sheet of plywood, position the saw above the cut line and place the front lip of the base down on the panel. Lift the saw forward and move the saw guard forward and away from the blade until the blade is well exposed. (Keep your fingers well away from the blade.) Then turn on the saw and slowly lower the blade back down and into the saw line. This makes a "plunge cut" directly into the material. You can cut a square from the center of a piece of plywood in this manner. But remember, you will have to go past the lines at the corners to complete the cut on the underside, or you can finish the cuts with a hand saw.

Portable Saber Saw

Another type of saw that is quite handy around the homestead is a portable saber saw. Normally this isn't used for a tremendous amount of rough framing cutting because it is smaller and takes more time to make cuts. It is more versatile than the circular saw and can be used to cut circular or irregular shaped pieces. There are a number of different types of blades available and they can be used for cutting anything from 2 x 4s, through fine plywood, stone, metal, or fiberglass to ceramic tile.

One chief advantage of a saber saw is that you can use it to cut a hole in a surface without first boring a starting hole. Merely tilt the saw forward on the front of its base until the blade stops touching the wood surface. Then start the saw and slowly lower it backward until the sawblade contacts the wood surface. Slowly continue lowering until the blade penetrates the wood surface. Then make the cut as needed.

Portable Electric Drill

In the number of tools sold, the portable electric drill is the most popular. And with good reason; not only can it be used for

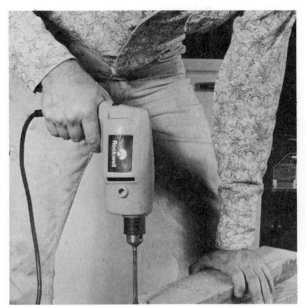

A variable-speed, portable electric drill; for safety, buy double-insulated model.

A convenient, safe model is the cordless portable drill, ideal for field work.

boring holes, it can be used as a power fastener for quick driving of screws, or small hex head screws. With the right accessories, it can be used to mix paint, even pump out a basement.

Again the drill must be double insulated. Although there are plenty of cheap drills on the market, a good-quality ⅜-inch, variable-speed, reversing drill is probably the best bet. Although it may cost a bit more, it can do a great deal more and will last a lifetime if cared for properly. An even better bet for the farm or garden is a cordless drill because you can carry it right to the job without the risk of accidental electric shock.

BITS. When using an electric drill for boring holes, it's important to choose the correct bit. Buy nothing but the best. For most work, good-quality, high-speed steel bits will do. Forget the cheap sets of bits sold in bargain bins. Good high-quality bits are expensive ($2 to $3 each); and my method is to purchase bits as I need them. By following this practice, I don't notice the cost as much.

For rough work or larger holes, pur-

chase spade bits. These are flat bits shaped much like a shovel blade, but with a sharp tip. When run at high speeds they will do a great job of cutting soft material such as soft framing woods. These bits must be kept sharp, which is fairly easy to do with a small file. Spade bits will jump around quite a bit when they break through the hole, so keep a good grip on the drill. (Again, it's a good idea to back the piece to be drilled with a piece of scrap wood. Drill through into the scrap, but not through it.) Above all, don't attempt to use bits (in an electric drill) such as auger bits or expansion bits that have screw tips on them. Not only will you ruin the work, but you may be injured.

In addition to the bits mentioned, you can also get carbide-tipped masonry bits used for drilling in masonry or concrete. Or you can get a hole saw, a circular cutter that cuts holes up to about three inches in diameter. These are great for cutting plumbing waste drain line holes, and for drilling holes for bird houses and door knobs. With other accessories, you can polish your car, grind off old paint or rust and do many other chores.

47

DRILL-PRESS ATTACHMENT. One of the best accessories for your electric drill is a small drill-press attachment. A drill press is just about the only way of boring precision holes you may need for repairing small tractors and farm machinery. With this device, your drill is clamped in the press and used as a stationary tool. When fitted with a variable speed drill these tools can be used for all but the most exacting metal work.

Their big disadvantage is they don't provide as much accuracy as does a full-size drill press, nor the amount of travel.

DRILL PRESS. A full-size drill press is a valuable stationary power tool. However, these are fairly expensive and the best bet is to watch newspaper ads for a used one or buy one at a farm auction. One with a tilting head is best.

A drill press is ideal for precision jobs such as boring through this joint.

Owning a drill press, which comes in many sizes, saves trips to the machine shop.

Radial Arm Saw

If you will be doing a lot of woodworking, such as building furniture or other fine items, you will want a radial arm saw. These are one of the most versatile of the stationary power tools. In effect, they are stationary circular saws. They can be used easily for cross-cutting or ripping. They can also be fitted easily with accessories such as a shaper cutter, disc and drum sander and used for other jobs. These tools are a big investment; make sure you can justify it before purchasing them.

SHOP SMITH. The old-time Shop Smith is a combination tool that allows you to have almost all the tools of a professional woodworking shop without devoting a lot of money or space to a large number of stationary tools. This tool combines five tools in one and it fits in a space about the same size as a bicycle. The tool can be used as a stationary table saw. The tool also includes a lathe, disc and drum sander, drill press and horizontal doweling machine. This is an old-time machine returned to use by popular demand, and it's one of the best buys for any woodworking shop. The only disadvantage is the time required to set the machine up. If set up as a saw and you need to drill a hole, then the saw must be dismantled and the machine set up as a drill press.

Belt Grinder

This is a small stationary tool used for everything from grinding down a metal surface to sharpening a pair of scissors or a pocketknife. It can be used for some wood sanding jobs as well. This tool has a small abrasive belt that runs around a couple of wheels. The belt passes through a table that can be tilted or kept flat. By changing the grit on the belt you can vary the abrasiveness of the tool.

You may not need some of the tools mentioned, or you may need others such as a *shaper*, which is used to shape edges on boards or to make molding. However, the tools mentioned will handle most any job around the farm or homestead. With most power tools, one or two good-quality, three-conductor extension cords are needed because many jobs are some distance from outlets. Remember, wire size is important: the longer the cord, the larger the wire diameter needed.

A radial arm saw is a must for furniture making or advanced woodworking.

The Shopsmith is a fine, all-purpose tool that may be stored in a small area.

A belt grinder is a stationary tool, well suited for sharpening and sanding.

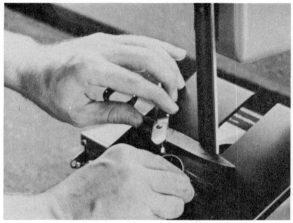

A belt grinder sharpens.

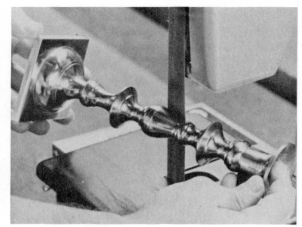

It cleans and polishes.

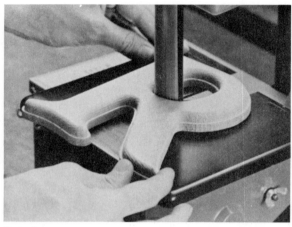

It sands.

It grinds and deburrs.

Chapter 4

How to Sharpen Almost Anything

I learned a long time ago that the safest and easiest tool to use is a sharp one. If you have to force a dull cutting tool of any kind, it can slip and cause a bad cut. One of my great uncles was an old-time woodsman and trapper, and he said, "The more time you spend sharpening a knife, the less time you'll spend using it." He spent many hours setting on his back porch step sharpening and honing not only his knives, but his carpenter's tools as well. You could shave the hair off your arm with one of his chisels.

There are literally hundreds of cutting tools used every day in the home, workshop, and on the lawn and garden. Each requires a different method of sharpening, but a little time spent learning how to sharpen them and keeping them sharp can mean the difference between a pleasant chore and utter frustration.

GRINDERS. There are many different kinds of tools that can be used to sharpen tools such as axes and hoes. The most commonly used tool is a *bench grinder* of some sort. This can be nothing more than

51

Powered bench grinder speeds sharpening.

shattering stone could cause serious injury.

Another type of grinder is the *belt grinder.* I consider it one of the handiest power tools in my shop. It can be used to grind almost anything from metal to wood to glass. It is safer than many other grinders, especially for first-timers. Instead of a wheel, it uses an abrasive belt for grinding. The table on the unit shown tilts to allow for sharpening even very shallow angle cuts such as thin-bladed fillet knives.

a spindle with bearings, a pulley in the middle, and a wheel on each end. The grinder is powered by an electric motor.

Some fancier ones have built-in motors, but they're expensive and, in my opinion, not as practical for the small farm as the spindle-type grinders. Fancier models may be a bit more accurate for grinding workshop tools and for special metal grinding. Two advantages of the spindle type of grinder are that it can be used with wire wheels to clean rust and dirt from tools, and it can be fitted with a special sickle bar sharpener. This is about the only way you can sharpen a sickle bar mower blade easily. Spindle-type grinders should have stone shields to protect the operator if a grindstone breaks. At more than 3,000 revolutions per minute, an unprotected,

Easy-to-use, multi-purpose belt grinder.

A specially-shaped sickle grinder wheel.

SAFETY. Anytime you're using an electric bench or belt grinder, wear safety goggles or a safety shield for your eyes. Be careful not to allow the tool being sharpened to become overheated; not only can you get a bad burn, you'll ruin the edge and there's a chance of a fire starting. It's a good idea to keep a fire extinguisher handy near the grinder in case a spark happens to ignite something.

When using a wheel-type grinder for larger tools such as axes, I prefer not to use the adjustable angle table and merely hold the tool in place. The tool being sharpened must be held about two-thirds the way down on the wheel and with the edge pointing down. Make sure you have a good grip on the tool.

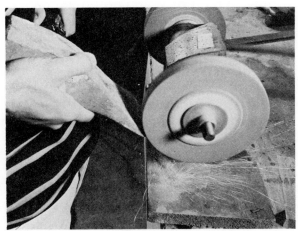

Hold tool so edge touches lower third of grinding wheel as shown.

For sharpening smaller tools, use the adjustable guide table to ensure proper cutting angles. A lot of sharpening can be done with a file. I use a good fine mill-cut bastard file for larger work and a small "locksmith" file for smaller work. You will also need small triangular files for sharpening saw blades.

Knives

Probably the most commonly sharpened tool is a knife of some sort. These may include thin-bladed fish filleting knives, kitchen knives, heavy-duty hunting knives, and even the old faithful pocketknife inherited from Dad. Regardless of what kind they are, they must be kept sharp, and that's not only an easy job, but fun. Many people think putting a good sharp edge on a knife is a mystery. It's not, but it does require time and patience.

FILING. I never use an electric grindstone to sharpen a knife. The thin blade can be ruined too easily by overheating. It's much easier to use a good mill-cut bastard file instead or, if you're lucky and can find one of the old time foot-operated grindstones, you can really do a good job on a knife edge. Hold the knife on a good solid surface with the edge of the blade facing away from you. Stroke by pushing the file across the edge and away from it, lifting the file after each stroke. Never drag the file against the edge. A good file can easily shape up even a badly nicked knife in a matter of minutes. File a little bit on one side, then turn the knife over and file on the opposite side.

Try to maintain the angle of the edge that has been put on the blade. Each knife has a different edge angle. A thin-bladed fish-filleting knife should normally be filed with about a five- to ten-degree sharpening angle. Kitchen knives and most hunting knives require about a 15-degree sharpening angle, while heavy duty utility knives can be sharpened as bluntly as 30 degrees. It's not necessary to maintain these angles exactly; they are recommended, though, both for sharpening and honing with a whetstone; if held at the recommended angles, each knife may be sharpened to its proper cutting edge. Don't remove any more material from the knife edge than is absolutely necessary.

HONING. After filing down the edge and removing nicks, the next step is to hone the edge on a good, smooth, Arkansas stone.* Many people don't understand how to hone knives properly. A couple of light strokes on a whetstone just won't put a razor sharp edge on a dull knife.

---

* Arkansas stones have an extremely fine grit and are often used for finish honing. Carborundum (used for various abrasives) stones are another possibility. They come in assorted grits.

The proper method of doing this is to secure the stone in a vise or hold it securely by some other means. Hold the knife handle in one hand with the edge facing away from you. Hold the back of the knife blade with the tips of the fingers of the other hand. Pull down with the hand holding the handle, and at the same time push forward with the opposite hand, making a downward sweeping stroke on the stone. Keep the stone well oiled with light machine oil and apply plenty of pressure on the back of the blade to sort of "slice off the stone," but not enough to bend the knife blade out of shape. Make a few strokes on one side, then turn the knife over and make a few strokes on the opposite. It takes patience and time to achieve an extremely sharp edge, but that's all there is to it. If you wish, you can make the blade even sharper. Drag it backward across the stone once or twice before finishing, then drag it backward across a piece of oiled leather such as the inside of an old belt.

TEST FOR SHARPNESS. Regardless of what old-timers do, never test the blade of a knife for sharpness by running your finger across the blade; if the blade has been properly sharpened, *it will cut.* One test for sharpness is to drag the blade across the top of your fingernail; if it slides smooth and nicks the nail, it's sharp. If it catches, back to the stone! An even safer method of testing is to hold a piece of newspaper and drag the knife blade across the edge of the newspaper. If the knife is sharp it will slice through the paper easily without tearing or snagging on the paper.

All sharpening, grinding and honing is done only on the small area of the edge. Grinding or honing marks high up on the blade do nothing for its sharpness, and they not only weaken the blade, but look terrible and indicate sloppy work.

Once a knife is sharpened properly, an occasional honing will keep it in good shape. Kitchen knives can be kept in good working order with a butcher's sharpening steel. Merely drag the edge across the steel, turn the knife over and drag the opposite side. Do several strokes on each side. Don't attempt the fancy flourishes of the butcher, but merely place the end of the steel against something solid and pull the knife blade slowly and carefully across the steel. Repeat these steps each time the knife is used.

To sharpen, hold knife firmly, push forward against edge and pull handle down.

Scissors

Completely different—and often neglected—are scissors, tinsnips, and other types of leverage-cutting tools. In many cases, you have to take the tool apart to do a good sharpening job; then sharpen each half, and rejoin the halves.

Again, my preference for sharpening these tools is a good file. Hold the scissor or tinsnip half on a firm surface and stroke away from the edge on the forward strokes, maintaining the angle. After filing the angled edge, turn the tool over and make one single stroke on the flat side to smooth up the edge.

If you really want to make Mom happy, complete sharpening the scissors by honing them as well, using carborundum stones lubricated with oil. Some pliers also may be sharpened in this manner, although you won't be able to separate the two halves. Use a small file to file down the angled edge on such pliers as side and end cutters.

Axes

Sharpening axes, mauls and hatchets is the next most common chore. A dull axe is one of the most dangerous tools you can use. It will glance rather than cut in, and a glancing axe can put you or someone close to you in a hospital. Unless the axe is badly chipped or nicked, I prefer to file it down rather than grind it. Most axe blades are pretty soft and this job goes fast.

Once all nicks have been removed from the edge, use a hone, preferably a small circular or axe stone, on the edge of the axe in a circular motion. Turn the blade several times during the honing to make sure it is sharpened uniformly.

One of the most common mistakes in sharpening an axe is to sharpen it to a concave edge. An axe that is properly sharp-ened should have a rounded, convex edge. This allows the axe to dig in, but also allows you to pull it out easily, and the "wedge" shape of the axe helps in the cutting process by forcing the wood fibers apart.

I like to sharpen one edge of a double-bitted axe fairly sharp, and with a bit more shallow angle. Then the other edge is kept pretty blunt. A spot of paint on the top of the handle near the head indicates the "dull" side. This side is used for "ground" work or cutting off trees or roots near the ground, keeping one side sharp for lopping off limbs out of danger of rocks.

A splitting maul is sharpened in the same manner, but the edge is kept more rounded, and is not honed. Many folks seem to think a splitting maul doesn't need to be sharpened, but I like to run mine over the grindstone once on each side just before using. It sort of takes some of the "roll" out of the edge and makes the maul bite in instead of bounce off wood such as blackjack oak. It's a good idea to carry a small pocket stone for on-the-spot sharpening of axes and knives while in the field. Some of the better ones will fit in a pouch on your belt.

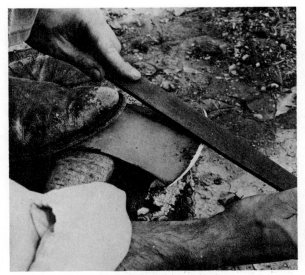

I try to keep one edge of a double bit axe extremely sharp, the other "rounded" for rough cutting.

A small hone is ideal for putting a sharp edge on an axe while in the field.

55

Grass Cutter

Another tool that gets a lot of use on the farm or around a garden is a grass hook or weed cutter. There are two basic types—one has a serrated edge and one doesn't. The one with the serrated edge must be sharpened by hand with the proper size file. The straight-edge cutter can be ground on a wheel or belt grinder. Grind only on the edge which has the angle ground on it. Keep the original angle as well as the slight concave surface to the cutter. Then use a file lightly across the back surface to knock off burrs on the edge caused by grinding and to give the cutter a smooth edge.

Hoe

A sharp hoe eases gardening. A dull hoe can make a fellow think of fishing faster than anything I can think of. If the edge of the hoe is nicked and rounded, use a coarse grinding wheel or belt grinder to cut it down to a wide angle as shown in the drawing. A small pocket file can be kept handy and used to touch up the hoe in the field.

To sharpen, hold hoe firmly as shown.

Pruning Shears

Pruning shears and tinsnips are sharpened the same way household scissors are sharpened. Again, remember to maintain the proper angle, and, on round-edged tools such as pruning shears, make sure you maintain the proper shape of the blade. The shears can be clamped in a vise and the edges can be sharpened with a good mill bastard file. Usually, separating the two halves is not necessary. Tools such

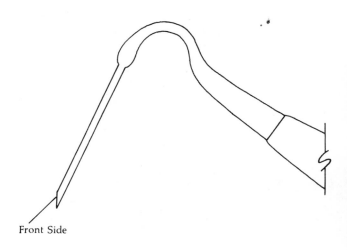

Front Side

Sharpen only the hoe's angled, front side.

Use vise to hold shears for sharpening.

as pruners are more easily sharpened while they're still together rather than when apart. Clamp in a good vise and use a file on them because it's easier to maintain the proper cutting angle on the rounded edge.

Lawn Mower Blades

Your power mower will do a much better job if the blade is kept sharp, and this is an easy matter, using a grindstone without a guide. Just remember to keep the blade moving to prevent overheating it. If you want to make sure you've got the blade balanced after sharpening, place a marble or round ball in a depression in a block of wood. Center the blade on this to determine which side needs a little more taken off.

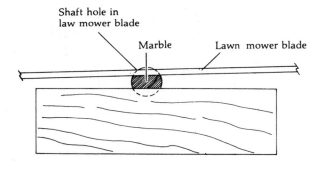

Shaft hole in
law mower blade

Marble   Lawn mower blade

Simple, home-made, blade-balancing device.

Sharpening Saws and Setting Teeth

For the homeowner with a workshop, or the guy who does his own gardening, there are lots of sharpening chores. Workshop saws must be kept sharp and, unless they're in extremely bad shape, they can easily be filed sharp at home. The main thing is to have the blade clamped securely and to use the proper size file for the

teeth of the saw. Each saw, from a pruning saw to a hand saw, has teeth with different sizes and configurations. Always maintain the proper filing angle, and stroke only away from the edge, not against it, again lifting the file between strokes. It's a good idea to file all sides of the teeth that go in one direction, turn saw around and file opposite sides of teeth. Count strokes on each tooth and try to make the same number and keep the same amount of pressure on each stroke. Pruning saws are easier to sharpen than hand saws because they have large, easily accessible teeth.

It's easy to sharpen handsaws, and, although it takes a bit of time and patience, it's well worth the effort. Whether it is a rip or crosscut saw, the teeth are "set," meaning that each alternate tooth is bent over in the opposite direction. This makes the saw kerf larger than the blade width and reduces friction, allowing the blade to pass through the cut easily. The teeth won't have to be reset each time you sharpen the saw, although it's not a bad idea to reset them every third or fourth time, or as needed.

The first step is to examine the saw to make sure that no teeth are missing. Examine the set: Do the teeth need to be reset? If so, place the saw in a handsaw vise, with the vise securely clamped to a solid work surface and at a comfortable working height. Make sure there is adequate lighting so you can see the teeth easily.

A device called a *saw tooth setter* is used to bend the teeth to the required set. This tool is shaped somewhat like a pair of funny looking pliers and is placed down over the tooth to be set. Squeezing the setter handle bends the tooth to produce the set. You must do every other tooth, then turn the saw around in the saw vice and do the opposite alternating teeth. Hand tooth setters are usually adjustable for the teeth or points per inch. It is very important that you produce the same amount of set or bend in each tooth, or you will produce a saw that will try to "crab" up and out of the line, producing a crooked line. The depth

For best results, use special saw vise and tooth setter to "set" or bend teeth the desired amount.

to which the tooth is set should not be more than half the tooth or the tooth may crack the blade in the gullet.

After the teeth have been set, the next step is to file them. On a ripsaw, the teeth are filed straight across like tiny chisels. On a crosscut saw, the teeth are filed at about a 45-degree angle to the blade. If the teeth are in pretty good shape, all they may need is touching up with the file. If some are broken or chipped, you'll have to "plane" them all down to one "height." This means filing across the tips to produce an even edge to the saw.

Place the saw in the saw vise so the teeth are about ¼ inch above the jaws. On a crosscut saw, examine the teeth to determine which teeth have which angles and file the alternative teeth as required. The file should file the front of one tooth and the back of another tooth at the same time. If the saw has been planed down, file to about the middle of the flat on top of the tooth. After all the alternating teeth have been filed one way, turn the saw and file the opposite alternating teeth in the opposite angle. The angle should be about 45 degrees to the saw blade positioned in the saw vice. Make sure that all teeth are filed evenly. The file must be held down in the gullet of the tooth and not be tilted one way or another.

To complete the saw sharpening job, file each tooth separately.

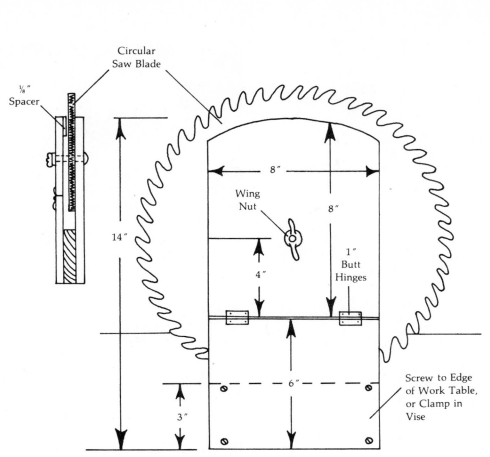

Circular saw blades may be sharpened in a home-built holder, made of standard-size stock and hardware. Dimensions of holder may be adjusted as necessary.

Bits

If you own a brace and bit, it can be much easier to use if the bits are kept sharp. Use a small file. My favorite is a small, flat, locksmith's file. File the flat ends first, maintaining the angle, then file the leading cutting edge. It normally doesn't take too much filing or pressure to sharpen these tools.

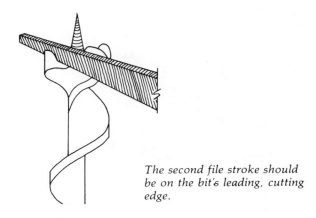

The second file stroke should be on the bit's leading, cutting edge.

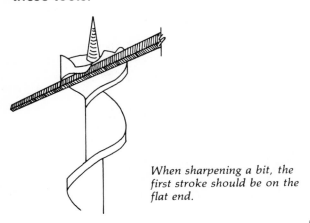

When sharpening a bit, the first stroke should be on the flat end.

You can also sharpen small portable electrically-driven bits with a file, but they're sharpened easier using an electric grindstone or belt grinder. Make sure you just touch the bit to the wheel, and that you maintain the proper angle. Don't allow the bit to remain on the wheel too long or the metal will overheat and the bit will loose its temper.

59

Chisels

When it comes to woodworking, one tool that must be kept absolutely sharp is the chisel. Both flat and round or "gouge" chisels may be sharpened easily on a grindstone, then honed to a fine cutting edge.

Again, the most important thing is to maintain the proper cutting angle, and not to allow the metal to become overheated. Move the chisel back and forth across the wheel while sharpening, and touch the chisel to the wheel with light strokes. Don't push the chisel up against the wheel and hold it firmly; you'll ruin it.

Flat chisels can be first ground to shape, then honed like a knife on a good stone. The final step in honing is to drag the flat, back portion of the chisel across the stone to knock off the edge caused by honing the beveled side.

Keep round chisel turning back and forth, grinding off just a bit at a time; maintain the angle as well as the roundness of the edge.

To put final outside edge on gouge, push tool against concave side of gouge stone.

Hold chisel edge down hard when sharpening on oil-dampened stone.

Round chisels can also be sharpened on the grindstone, but make sure you keep turning the chisel to maintain the rounded edge, as well as the correct cutting angle. To put a good sharp edge on a rounded chisel or gouge, you'll need a special stone. Use the concave side of the stone to hone the outside rounded edge, then turn the stone over and drag the gouge back across the convex side to finish the sharpening.

Screwdrivers

Probably the most neglected tool in the shop is the screwdriver. When a screwdriver becomes old, battered, with rounded edges, or in the case of a "Phillips," with all four edges rounded, it should be sharpened. This not only makes it much easier to work hard-to-turn screws, but lessens the chance of marring the screw head as well. Use a file to tone up Phillips head screwdrivers. A regular flat-slot screwdriver can be sharpened easily on a grindstone. Make sure you keep the front edge absolutely square and flat. In fine or delicate work, such as gunsmithing, you'll often need a screwdriver to fit a specific screw. This prevents the chance of marring the screw. I always keep several extra screwdrivers around just for this purpose, and I grind them to suit a particular job.

Chapter 5   Welding

Without welding tools you will be lost on the farm or homestead. This is especially true if you live some distance from a town or professional welder. Learning to weld isn't particularly hard, but it does take a bit of practice and a great deal of attention to safety rules.

Basically there are two types of welding for the homesteader: *arc welding* and *oxyacetylene welding.*

For all practical purposes, either will suffice. However, equipment used in oxyacetylene welding is portable and can be taken into the field, whereas arc welding usually requires a stationary welder in a shop. There are gasoline motor–powered welders, but these are too expensive for the average homeowner or farmer.

One good rule is to install an arc welder near the shop door. Then you can pull a tractor or piece of equipment to the welder for repairs.

There have been entire books and even correspondence courses written on the subject of welding, and, of course, we can't cover that much material here. However, the basics are fairly simple, and with a little practice you will be able to do most of the welding jobs around your farm or homestead.

We will start with arc welding because the initial set up costs less and it is a bit easier for the "first-timer" to do than oxyacetylene welding.

ARC WELDING BASICS

1. The first rule is to carefully read the instruction manual that comes with your welder and follow all safety rules. Protect yourself from shock by adhering to the following safety rules:

A. Never allow contact between the "hot" parts of the circuits and bare skin or wet clothing. The electrode and work (or the ground) are electrical circuits that are "hot" when the welder is on. Always wear dry, hole-free gloves to protect and insulate your hands.

B. Never touch the electrically operating hot parts of two welders at the same time.

C. Never dip an electrode holder in water for cooling.

D. Keep yourself insulated from damp ground, especially when welding in damp locations.

E. Make sure the electrode holder, ground clamp, welding cable and machine are in good working order.

F. If working above ground make sure you are protected from a fall should you get an accidental shock. Keep electrode cable away from your body.

2. Arcburn can be more severe than a sunburn. To prevent:

A. Use a shield with the proper filter and cover plates to protect your eyes from the sparks and rays of the arc. The filter lens should be a No. 10, 11, or 12 and should conform to the ANSI Z87.1 standards.

B. Wear suitable clothing to protect yourself from metal splatters or rays from the arc.

C. Warn other people nearby about the dangers to their eyes and skin.

3. Make sure garments are oil free and that they protect you from the droplets of molten slag and metal thrown from the welding. Wear leather gloves and a heavy shirt with the sleeves rolled down completely. Wear a cap over your hair and earplugs if necessary.

4. When slag chipping, wear safety glasses.

5. Remove all fire hazards from the area, or cover them with a non-flammable material if they can't be removed.

6. When you are not welding, place the electrode holder where it is insulated from the ground system. Accidental grounding can cause overheating and is a fire hazard.

7. Make sure the welding work cable is attached to the work as close to the welding site as possible.

8. Avoid breathing welding fumes and provide plenty of ventilation. This is particularly important when welding galvanized, lead, or cadmium-plated steel and other metals which produce toxic fumes.

9. Don't weld in locations near chlorinated hydrocarbon vapors from cleaning, degreasing or spraying operations. These produce a highly toxic gas when combined with welding heat and rays.

10. Don't cut, heat, or weld tanks, drums or containers until all proper steps have been taken to insure that such procedures will not cause problems with flammable or toxic vapors from the substances inside. They can cause an explosion even though they have been "cleaned." For more information on this, purchase "Safe Practices For Welding and Cutting Containers That Have Held Combustibles," A6-0-65, from the American Welding Society, 2501 NW 7th Street, Miami, Florida 33125.

11. Vent hollow casting or containers so they don't explode during heating.

Equipment

There are several small home-shop type AC arc welders on the market. Some, such as those sold by the Lincoln Electric Co., are quite good. Some of the "cheapies" are worse than nothing. You can also purchase an AC-DC arc welder useable with either type of current. The single AC arc welder is less expensive and will suffice for most home welding jobs.

Most small shop welding outfits have from 225 to 295 amps and their cost increases with the number of amps. The welder shown is a 225. These welders come with cable and a three-prong male plug along with the appropriate female plug. These welders must be wired into a 220- to 250-volt line using the three incoming wires. Before installing, check with the power company to make sure you have adequate power for the welder. Either have a qualified electrician install the wiring or do it yourself if you know how and local codes allow it. The receptacle for the welder must be connected to the 220- to 250-line at the circuit breaker or fuse box using three No. 10 or larger copper wires in conduit. For long runs of more than 100 feet, No. 8 wire should be used. The two hot lines must be fused with 50-ampere super lag fuses. The center contact in the receptacle is for the grounding connection. The green wire in the input cable connects this contact to the frame of the welder. This insures proper grounding of the welder frame when the welder plug is inserted into the receptacle. Make sure there is adequate air circulation around the welder.

In addition, the basic welder will also need a welding helmet and electrodes. In almost all cases of home welding, you will use general-purpose electrodes such as Fleetwood 180. The thickness of the metal

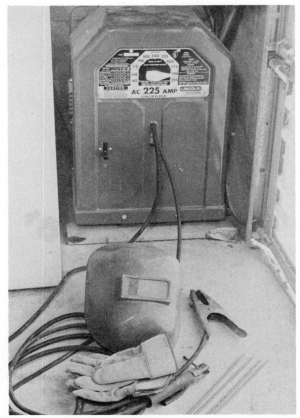

Typical small shop, 225-amp arc welder with accessories for safe operation.

to be welded and other factors determine the welding rod size and the amperes used.

PREPARING FOR WORK. Ready the work for welding as per your specific machine's instructions. Place the work on a good nonflammable surface. Clamp if necessary. A steel table makes a good welding table, especially one with an open top.

One thing you can't do is learn to weld by merely reading a book. You have to practice to be able to do it. Welding is much like riding a bicycle. At first it seems impossible. But all of a sudden it seems to just happen and you are amazed at how simple it is. On the other hand, to do a really good welding job takes practice and experience.

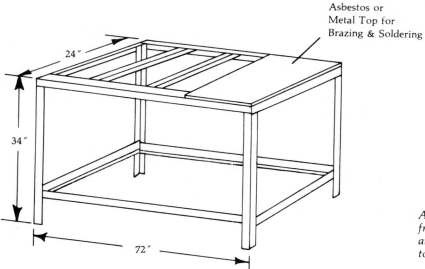

Asbestos or
Metal Top for
Brazing & Soldering

24″

34″

72″

A welding table may be made from 1 × 1-inch angle iron and a metal top, soldered together.

ELECTRODE IDENTIFICATION AND OPERATING DATA

The current ranges given represent minimum and maximum metered currents for which each electrode is designed.

Actual machine setting is influenced by plate thickness, joint position and operator preference.

COATING COLOR	Conforms to Test Requirements of AWS Class	ELECTRODE BRAND NAME	ELECTRODE POLARITY (+) = "REVERSE" (−) = "STRAIGHT"	5/64″ SIZE	3/32″ SIZE	1/8″ SIZE	5/32″ SIZE	3/16″ SIZE	7/32″ SIZE	1/4″ SIZE	5/16″ SIZE
MILD STEEL											
Light Tan	E6010	Fleetweld 5	DC (+)						200-275	250-325	280-400
Brick Red	E6010	Fleetweld 5P	DC (+)		40-75	75-130	90-175	140-225			
Tan	E6012	Fleetweld 7	DC (−)			80-135	110-180	155-250	225-290	245-325	
			AC			90-150	120-200	170-275	250-320	275-360	
Light Tan	E6011	Fleetweld 35	AC			75-120	90-160	120-200	150-260	180-300	
			DC (+)			70-110	80-145	110-180	135-235	170-270	
Red Brown	E6011	Fleetweld 35LS	AC			80-130	120-160				
			DC (±)			70-120	110-150				
Dark Tan	E6013	Fleetweld 37	AC		75-105	100-150	150-200	200-260			
			DC (±)		70-95	90-135	135-180	180-235			
Gray-Brown	E7014	Fleetweld 47	AC			110-160	150-225	200-280	260-340	280-425	
			DC (−)			100-145	135-200	180-250	235-305	260-380	
Brown*	E6013	Fleetweld 57	AC	45-80	75-105	100-150	150-200	200-260	250-310	300-360	360-460
			DC (±)	40-75	70-95	90-135	135-180	180-235	225-280	270-330	330-430
Brown	E6011	Fleetweld 180	AC			40-90	60-120	115-150			
			DC (+)			40-80	55-110	105-135			
Gray	E7024	Jetweld®1	AC		65-120	115-175	180-240	240-300	300-380	350-440	
			DC (±)		60-110	100-160	160-215	220-280	270-340	320-400	
Brown	E6027	Jetweld 2	AC				190-240	250-300	300-380	350-450	
			DC (±)				175-215	230-270	270-340	315-405	
Gray*	E7024	Jetweld 3	AC			115-175	180-240	240-315	300-380	350-450	450-600
			DC (±)			100-160	160-215	215-285	270-340	315-405	
Gray	E7018	Jetweld LH-70	DC (+)		70-100	90-150	120-280	170-280	210-330	290-430	375-500
			AC		80-120	110-170	135-225	200-300	260-380	325-440	400-530
Gray*	E7018	Jet LH®72	DC (+)		70-100	85-150	120-190	190-260			
			AC		80-120	100-170	135-225	180-280			
Gray-Brown	E7028	Jetweld LH-3800	AC				180-270	240-330	275-410	360-520	
			DC (+)				170-240	210-300	260-380		

It's a good idea to get ahold of some ³⁄₁₆-inch or heavier, low-carbon steel plate and practice different types of welds on this "scrap." To be able to weld you must master four things: the correct welding position, the correct way to strike an arc, the correct arc length, and the correct welding speed. Speed changes according to the type of welding or metal.

Welding Techniques

THE CORRECT POSITION. If you are right handed, hold the electrode holder in your right hand and bring the left hand to the underside of the right hand to increase steadiness. Then pull the left elbow into your left side. Hold the electrode at a slight angle and weld from left to right. If you are left handed, reverse the entire procedure.

STRIKING AN ARC. Probably the hardest thing for most beginning welders to do is to strike an arc. The most common mistake is to jab at the metal with the electrode. This often causes the rod to stick to the metal once the arc is begun.

First, lower your head shield. Then scratch the electrode slowly across the surface of the metal. As you see the sparks flying, lift the electrode about ⅛ of an inch to establish the arc. Never stop the electrode once you start scratching it across the metal surface. Doing so will cause the electrode to stick to the metal.

THE CORRECT ARC LENGTH. The arc length is the distance from the tip of the electrode core wire to the base metal. In order to weld properly this distance must be properly maintained. The distance should be short, from ¹⁄₁₆ to ⅛ of an inch. As the electrode burns off it must be fed toward the work to keep the arc the proper length. The sound the arc makes is an important indication. If the arc is of the proper length, there will be a popping, crackling sound much like eggs frying in a skillet. If the arc is too long, the sound will be more hollow and sound like a hiss.

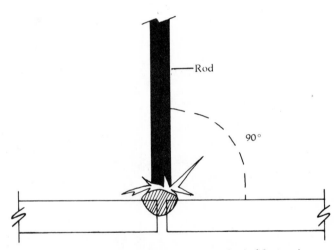

From side, electrode should appear to be held straight.

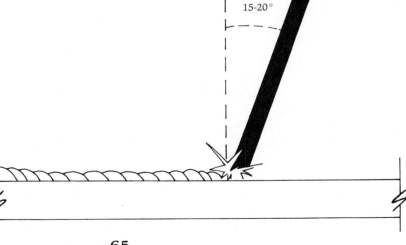

Electrode or rod (front view) at correct angle for laying bead. Hold rod about ⅛-inch off metal to maintain arc.

65

WELDING SPEED. Maintaining the correct welding speed consistently is hard to learn. Different speeds are necessary for different metals and heats.

To maintain the proper speed you must watch the puddle of molten metal right behind the arc instead of watching the arc. Watching the arc is a common beginners' mistake. The appearance of the puddle gives an indication of the welding speed. The ridge where the molten puddle of metal solidifies should be approximately 3/8 of an inch behind the electrode. Most beginners weld too fast, resulting in a thin and uneven bead.

Ridge Where
Metal Solidifies

Molten Metal

If ridge where molten metal solidifies is about 3/8 of an inch behind rim of rod, welding speed is correct.

Another common beginners' mistake is to weave the electrode back and forth. For most general welding, this isn't necessary. Merely weld along at a steady even pace and in a nice straight line. The thinner the metal plate, the faster you have to weld.

YOUR FIRST PRACTICE SESSION. Use the mild steel plate 3/16 of an inch or heavier, a 1/8-inch Fleetwood 180 electrode and set the current at 105 amps on the welder.

Position the electrode holder correctly and drop your face shield in place. Scratch the electrode across the surface of the steel plate to start the arc. Practice several times until you can strike an arc correctly and consistently. Then start moving the arc, slowly welding from left to right (if right handed).

Practice running beads across the plate. It's a good idea to run a practice bead about an inch from the top of the plate and across it. Then run one about an inch below this one. This gives you a chance to practice making straight beads. Remember to watch the molten metal puddle as you go.

Most metals to be welded around the farm or home shop are low carbon and are often called "mild steel." Usually, this type of steel doesn't cause too much trouble. Some steels, however, such as those used for plowshares, axles and connecting rods, are made of higher carbon. These must be preheated and require a great deal of care in welding. Stay away from these until you become proficient with lower carbon steels. The main thing is to get a good quality weld that will be free of oil, paint, and rust. If done properly, the weld will be stronger than the metal itself.

Weld Joints

There are five basic welding joints: butt, fillet, lap, edge and corner.

BUTT WELD. This is probably the most commonly used type of weld. An example of this would be to place two metal plates side by side with about a 1/16-inch spacing between them. Then "tack weld" the plates together on each end. If you don't, the heat will force the plates apart as shown. After tacking, begin welding the two plates together from the left to the

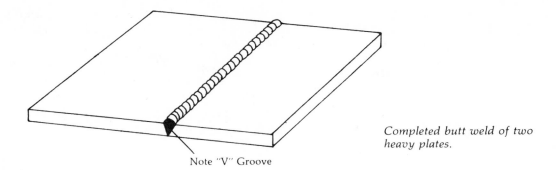

Note "V" Groove

Completed butt weld of two heavy plates.

right hand side (if right handed). Place the point of the electrode down in the crack between the two plates and keep it slightly tilted in the direction of travel.

Make sure the molten metal spreads evenly on both sides of the plates. For a better joint, it is a good idea to grind a bevel on the plate edges. A good weld penetrates the joint completely. Shown are examples of both good and bad butt joint welds.

When welding heavy plate with a butt weld, make successive passes to fill in the V groove formed by grinding down the edges.

The *lap weld, edge weld* and *corner weld* are fashioned in a manner similar to that used for the butt weld.

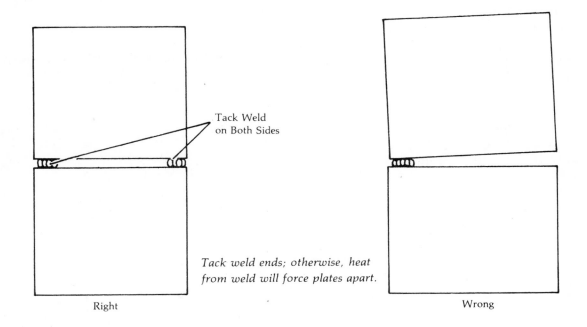

Tack Weld on Both Sides

Tack weld ends; otherwise, heat from weld will force plates apart.

Right

Wrong

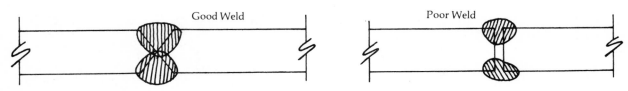

Good Weld

Poor Weld

When welding a butt weld, bevel edges and position pieces as shown at left.

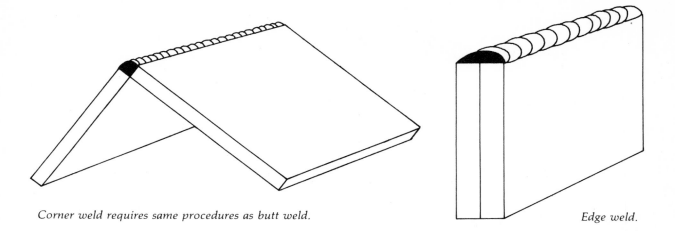

Corner weld requires same procedures as butt weld.

Edge weld.

FILLET WELD. The single most important factor in welding fillet joints is to keep the electrode at a 45-degree angle between the two sides. Otherwise the metal won't distribute itself evenly on both sides of the joint. The best method of holding the rod at the angle is to place the electrode in the holder at a 45-degree angle.

Fillet welds must be of a minimum thickness as shown in the chart. Anytime two pieces of different thickness are joined always make the fillet weld size to suit the thickest material.

When multiple passes are required to fill a thick fillet, place the first bead in the corner with a fairly high current and disregard the undercut. Then fill in with the filler beads, applying the last bead against the vertical plate.

Minimum Fillet-Weld Size

The minimum sizes of fillet welds for specific material thicknesses are shown below. Where materials of different thicknesses are being joined, the minimum fillet weld size is governed by the thicker material.

Material Thickness of Thicker Part Joined (in.)		Minimum Fillet Size (in.)
to ¼ incl.		⅛
over ¼	to ½	³⁄₁₆
over ½	to ¾	¼
over ¾	to 1½	⁵⁄₁₆
over 1½	to 2¼	⅜
over 2¼	to 6	½
over 6		⅝

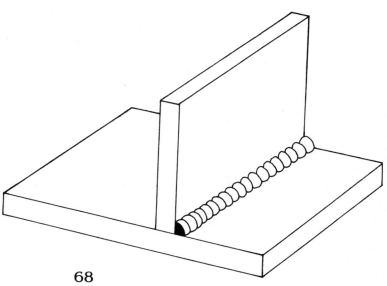

Fillet weld. Use chart above as guide for minimum fillet-weld sizes.

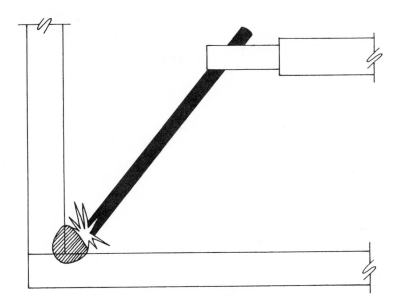

When making fillet welds, the electrode is usually placed in the holder at a 45° angle.

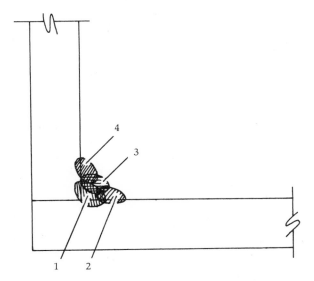

Apply welds in sequence shown, as necessary, to make up the fillet.

Welding Vertically

In many cases you may have to weld a vertical surface. This can be done in two ways: vertical up and vertical down welding.

VERTICAL "UP" WELDING. This is a hard type of welding to master because you need just enough molten metal to make the joint; if there's too much, it will drip or roll downward. The big problem is keeping the molten metal in place. However, using a few special techniques, this can be accomplished fairly easily with a little practice.

Use a ⅛-inch Fleetwood 180 electrode and an amp setting of 90 to 105. Keep the electrode horizontal or pointing slightly upward and deposit the metal at the bottom of the edge of the joint. Before you get too much metal deposited move the arc up about ½ to ¾ of an inch. This removes the heat from the molten puddle which then solidifies. This motion should be very slight and with the wrist only, not the entire arm. If done properly, you will create a long arc that deposits no metal, but keeps the arc going. During this process watch the molten metal only. *Don't watch the arc.* Then bring the arc back to the top edge of the molten metal and deposit another puddle. The entire operation should be done with slow, deliberate movements.

VERTICAL "DOWN" WELDING. This is a fast, shallow type of bead and is most often used when welding sheet metal.

Again use a ⅛-inch rod and, on thin metal, a 60- to 75-amp setting. Hold the electrode in a 30- to 45-degree angle with the tip pointing upward. Keep a very short

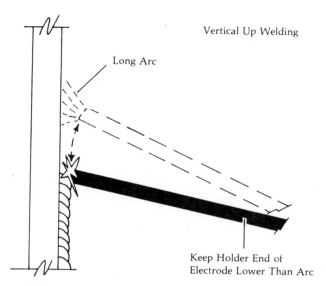

Vertical Up Welding

Long Arc

Keep Holder End of
Electrode Lower Than Arc

*When vertical "up" welding, move wrist slowly and
deliberately to lift electrode tip away from molten
metal. This allows metal to cool, while arc is maintained.*

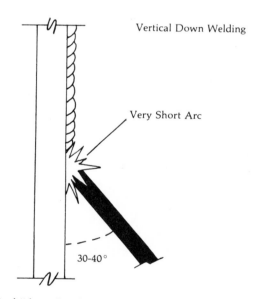

Vertical Down Welding

Very Short Arc

30-40°

*In vertical "down" welding, work quickly and main-
tain a very short arc.*

arc, but don't allow the electrode to touch
the metal. As the bead forms, continue
lowering the entire arm as the weld is
made so you maintain the correct angle.
By whipping the rod up and down slightly
you can prevent burning through on thin
metal.

Overhead Welding

You may have to do an occasional overhead welding job, but this is a chore you
should avoid if possible. A few tips will
make the job a bit easier. First, protect
yourself from flying sparks and any dripping molten metal. The primary thing is to
keep a very short arc (about ¹⁄₁₆ of an inch).
This will help keep the molten metal in
place. A long arc allows the metal to drop
away. Watch the molten puddle very
closely and, if necessary, use a slight back
and forth motion along the seam to help
prevent dripping of the metal. Another tip
is to place the electrode in the holder so it
sticks straight out. Then hold the electrode at an angle approximately 30 degrees off vertical.

In addition to normal welding you may
also need to weld sheet metal or cast iron.
These are hard to do and require special
techniques.

Welding Sheet Metal

When welding thin sheet metal, use lap
welds where possible because this provides more thickness. Weld fast and keep
the heat from staying too long in one spot.
Use a very short arc and ⅛-inch 180 electrode with an amperage of 75.

Welding Cast Iron

Welding cast iron is extremely hard for beginners. What usually happens is the heat
makes the surrounding metal brittle and
causes it to break near the weld. About the
only method for home welding of cast iron
is to weld not more than half an inch at a
time. Then allow this to cool completely
before welding any more on the seam.

Weld the next half an inch starting half
an inch away from the previous bead and
welding into it, then allow this to cool.

After welding you may wish to place the piece in sand to allow it to cool slowly.

It's a good idea to grind beveled edges on all cast iron welding joints if possible.

Cutting

An arc welder can be used easily for cutting through steel and cast iron. Use a ⅛-inch or ⁵⁄₃₂-inch 180 Fleetwood electrode and set the amperage at maximum on the welder.

Start the arc on the edge of the metal and hold a long arc until the metal melts through. Then push the arc through the molten metal allowing it to fall away. Raise the electrode and start again. Repeat this until the metal is cut. If a lot of cutting is being done you might wish to dip the electrode in water for a minute or two to allow it to cool. You may wish to shut down the welder first. This makes the electrode last longer.

You can pierce holes in metal quite easily as well. Again use the same electrode and maximum settings. Start the arc and hold the electrode in position and perpendicular to where you wish the hole. Keep a long arc (about ³⁄₁₆ of an inch), and when the metal becomes molten push the electrode down through the molten metal.

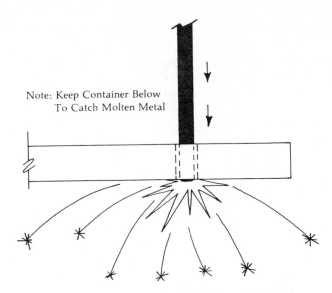

Note: Keep Container Below To Catch Molten Metal

To make hole, strike arc, then hold electrode still; as metal becomes molten, push electrode down. To enlarge hole, move electrode in circular motion.

Allow the molten metal a chance to fall through the hole. After making the initial hole use the electrode around the outside edge of the hole to enlarge the hole to the desired size.

Oxyacetylene Welding

Welding with oxyacetylene equipment is usually quite a bit harder for the beginner to master; however, it does have certain advantages: Welding techniques are quite a bit more versatile and a greater variety of jobs can be accomplished with this equipment than with arc welding equipment. You can sometimes take the equipment right in the field for repair jobs away from your shop.

Some disadvantages are: You must master both the welding torch and the welding rod at the same time, and this takes skill. In most instances, the equipment costs more than that for arc welding.

You will need a welding torch and a cutting attachment. These come packaged in sets including all other necessary items for

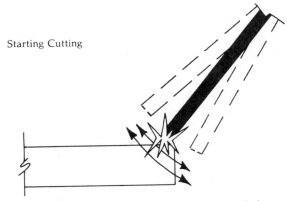

Starting Cutting

To start cutting, use a long arc at the edge of the metal. As the edge melts, raise the electrode and repeat the process.

71

most basic welding—goggles, regulators and hoses, etc.

In most cases, you will have to rent the cylinders of both oxygen and acetylene. These tanks contain gas at an extremely high pressure; and a lot of precautions are necessary for safe and proper operation. The number one rule is to *make sure the cylinders are kept where they can't be tipped over or dropped.* Any time a cylinder is not in use, or is to be moved, the cap for the cylinder must be screwed in place. Check local community and fire codes for storage rules for the tanks. Generally, they should be stored at room temperature; never store in high-temperature areas.

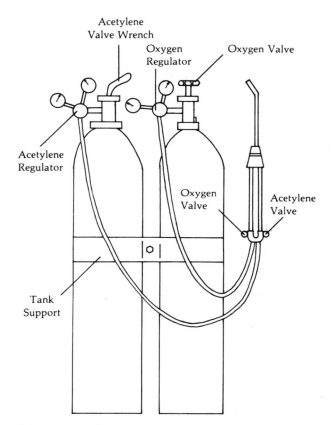

Basic oxyacetylene welding equipment.

SAFETY RULES. The same safety precautions mentioned for arc welding apply to oxyacetylene welding, and a few special safety rules should also be adhered to:

1. Wear the appropriate goggles with the special shades for the particular welding job you will be doing.

2. Wear leather gloves.

3. Make sure area surrounding work is fireproof.

4. Make sure no flammables or combustibles are around.

5. If possible, wear clothes without cuffs or pockets.

6. Keep all oxygen equipment free of oil or grease.

7. When checking for a leak, use soap. (Brush soapy water over connections; watch for bubbles.) If you discover a leak, don't use the equipment. Have it repaired, or call the equipment supplier.

8. Open oxygen valves slowly and stand to one side when opening all regulators, but open fully for use.

9. Make sure all oxygen lines, valves, regulators, etc., are purged before use.

10. The torch flame should be on only when you're holding the torch, otherwise turn off the flame.

11. If hose becomes burned or damaged, replace it; never tape it to repair it.

12. Always use a spark torch lighter to light torch.

13. Anytime you hear a shrill hissing sound, shut off tank immediately. This is called "flashback" and is dangerous. In most cases it is caused by a dirty tip, which you should remove and clean.

WELDING TORCH. A welding torch consists of a hand-held unit which contains a valve for the oxygen and the acetylene, plus a changeable tip that can be replaced with different-size tips for different jobs. This is connected to the gas cylinders by hoses that run to a regulator and cylinder valve on each cylinder. Before attaching your unit to the cylinders make sure you read the instructions that come with the unit and know exactly how to connect it to the cylinders, know how to use that particular unit and read all safety rules for it. You will probably be able to do most homeowner jobs by following information supplied with a kit.

Learn to adjust the torch correctly to achieve the right flame. In most cases this will be a neutral flame. After you have learned how to light and handle the equipment according to the instructions for your unit, the next step is to learn to "puddle." This is extremely important for torch welding.

WELDING METHODS. Most welding is done in the *forehand method,* which means the flame covers an area ahead of the welding bead and you work forward. The torch must be kept moving in a continuous motion, yet at the same time the cone of the flame must be kept in the edge of the "puddle" (a pool of molten metal). In order to learn to weld in this manner you must learn to run a bead of molten metal along a metal surface. This is done without the addition of welding rods. The width of the puddle gives an indication of its depth. Practice this operation on a piece of ³⁄₁₆-inch mild steel until you can weld a straight bead across the piece. The bead should not only be straight, but also consistent in size.

The main thing in creating a good puddle is that the very tip of the inner core of the flame must be kept within the little circle that is the molten metal at the end of the bead. This will normally be from ¹⁄₁₆ to ¹⁄₈ of an inch. The torch should be held at an angle of 30 to 45 degrees to the surface of the metal to be welded. The main thing is to learn to puddle without melting a hole through the metal, and yet achieve good penetration with the weld.

In many cases, you can weld without the use of welding rods merely by puddling the surface. A prime example is shown on the outside corner joint. When welding in

Torch flame adjustment: A. Open acetylene valve a bit; use spark lighter to ignite gas; B. Continue turning acetylene valve open until flame jumps away from tip when torch is shaken; or . . . C. When turbulence forms about ¾ to 1 inch in front of torch tip; D. Then slowly open oxygen valve; E. And continue turning valve until center flame is eliminated and the small flame becomes a small, rounded cone.

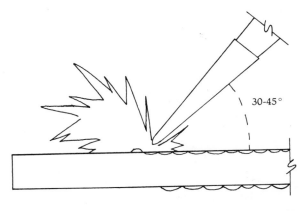

Hold torch at 30- to 45-degree angle. Keep cone in the "puddle" edge.

this manner, provide a bit of extra metal to be used as the filler. Welding without rods is normally done only on outside corner welds or those where you can provide plenty of filler metal from the parent pieces. However, in some cases you may also have to use molten metal from welding rods to fill in the weld, otherwise it may be too thin.

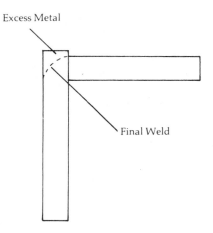

Outside corner joint: excess metal cut from edge may be used for weld.

Torch and welding rod are used to weld metal rods, joined at right angles.

WELDING WITH RODS. Welding with a rod is tricky. You must not only learn to operate the welding rod properly to create the puddle between the two pieces, but must also learn to bring the welding rod in at the proper time and apply it to fill in the seam. The idea is to create the puddle first, then bring in the welding rod to within about ⅛ of an inch from the surface of the puddle. It should be about ⅜ of an inch from the flame of the torch. It will soon become preheated and can then be dipped in the puddle where it will melt and begin to fill in the bead.

Allow only enough to melt to fill in the puddle, and bring it up to a slightly rounded surface. As soon as you melt enough metal, move the rod out to the outer edge of the surface as before to keep it preheated. This is where the tricky part comes in. If you withdraw the rod too far from the heat, it will cool rapidly and when you bring it back in it will cool the puddle,

making for a rough, uneven welding job. In the opposite extreme, if you keep it too close to the torch tip, drops of molten metal will splatter away from it and out of the puddle and onto the colder surrounding metal, again resulting in a poor weld.

One prime rule is once you start with one size rod on a weld, continue with the same size. It's much easier to maintain the same weld and feel for the rod in this manner.

It takes plenty of practice with a torch and rod to get a good weld with proper penetration, fusion and a good looking bead. To do it properly, you must maintain a consistent forward and circular motion with the torch, keep it at the proper angle, and at the same time feed the rod in properly with the opposite hand.

The welds for oxyacetylene welding are the same as for arc welding, butt, fillet, etc. And the same basic procedures for a good weld are necessary such as beveling the edges of a plate. If necessary to weld a wide joint, use one or more layers of bead

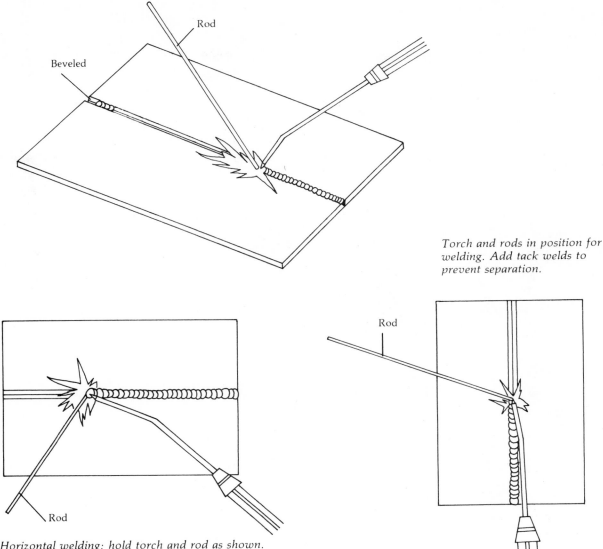

Beveled

Rod

Torch and rods in position for welding. Add tack welds to prevent separation.

Rod

Horizontal welding: hold torch and rod as shown. Point tip of rod slightly up.

Rod

Vertical welding with rod, torch in place.

to fill in and complete the joint. Naturally, it's much easier to weld in a "down flat" position, but this isn't always possible. Sometimes you will be required to weld in a horizontal position. This should be done as shown, with the tip of the torch pointing up just a bit.

Vertical welding is done from the bottom up, pointing the torch tip in the up position at about a 30-degree angle to the plate. Use very little torch motion for this type of welding.

Overhead welding with a torch is best left to the pros.

Oxyacetylene Cutting

Cutting metal with an oxyacetylene torch is similar to welding with the torch. In theory, the flame is used to heat the metal, then an oxygen jet is used to do the actual cutting. Most "welding and cutting" outfits sold for home use contain a separate cutting attachment for the torch. The oxyacetylene flame is used to heat the metal to

75

a cherry red, then the cutting lever is depressed to activate a separate oxygen jet. As the cut is made, the torch is moved along the line to be cut. The only thing you have to remember is that there will be a fairly wide kerf or slot left where the cut has been made, depending on the thickness of the metal being cut.

BRAZING AND SOLDERING. You may be called on frequently to braze or solder around the homestead. To braze, heat the parts to be mended, then dip a brazing rod in flux (powder that cleans metal surfaces and helps the brass rod adhere to the metal surface) and hold near the flame and parts to be mended. The brass rod will melt and join the two parts together. Soldering is done in much the same manner except it requires less heat and soft solder, an alloy of tin and lead, is used to join the metals.

Brazing or small soldering jobs are easy with this Oxygen-mapp torch.

Chapter 6

Refitting Old Tools With New Handles

Not too many years ago when you broke the handle of a rake, hoe or hammer, you got another at the nearby general or hardware store and repaired the tool. Today, when a handle breaks, many good tools get discarded. With a little searching you can find a handle that will fit almost anything, and with the back to basics movement not only are there more unusual old tools coming out of retirement, but many companies are again starting to make such tools as broad axes, cotton and strawberry hoes.

Check with your local hardware store or building supply dealer. Even if he doesn't have the handle you need he can probably order it for you. If you're lucky and find a hardware dealer with a good stock of handles, ask to look them over yourself instead of merely taking the first one he hands you. New handles are big business and they're made on production turning machines. They're not at all alike. Some may have big knots in them, others may be warped or even cut crooked. Others may have a bit of sapwood down one side. Be choosy, because if you don't you'll probably have to come back for another handle. Make sure the handle is solid, straight and without any knots or defects.

It's also a good idea to check for finish. An unfinished handle can be mighty rough on the hands.

Make sure you have the proper handle for your tool. Some handles, particularly those for axes and some shovels, can be confusing. It's not a bad idea to take the tool with you when shopping for a handle. Different shovel ferrules are bent differently and unless you pick a handle with the matching bend you'll be in trouble. Almost all handles are cut a bit oversize, but don't let that worry you. You can dress the wood down a bit to fit the tool. You can't, however, add wood if you find a handle that is too small to properly fit your tool.

Even if you have a tool with a handle that is not broken, but is cracked or loose, you may be better off with a new handle. Often with some kinds of tools, if the handle is merely loose you can tighten it with a new wedge. If the tool is very old, however, the wood may be so dry and crumbly that the new wedge won't hold and may make the tool even more dangerous. A head may fly off suddenly and injure someone. If, on the other hand, the handle is solid but loose, a new wedge can repair the tool.

Hammers

The first step, regardless of what type of hammer, is to choose the correct size handle to fit your hammer. The head end of the handle may be oversize, but the handle length and shape should conform to the old handle.

To remove the old handle, cut off flush with the bottom of the hammer head. Then place the head in a vise and drive out the remaining wood, driving around but not hitting the metal wedge. You may need to drill the wood first to loosen it. If this is the case, bore holes around the wedge, then drive out the loosened wood pieces. Use a drawknife or disc sander to shape the new handle end to fit, then drive it in place. Cut off any wood that protrudes above the head of the hammer and drive the wedges in place.

If a handle is cracked or broken, it must be removed. The first step is to cut off the handle up near the head of the tool.

78

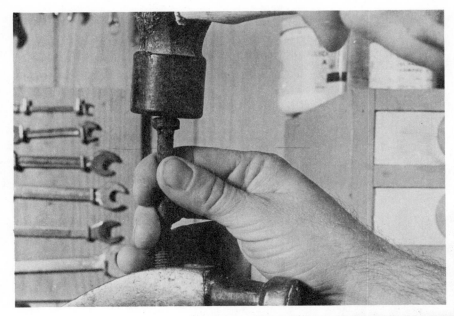

Using a flat-faced punch drive out the wood from around the metal wedge. Drive from the top of the head down. An old bolt makes an excellent tool for this job. You may also have to bore a few holes in the wood to loosen it up.

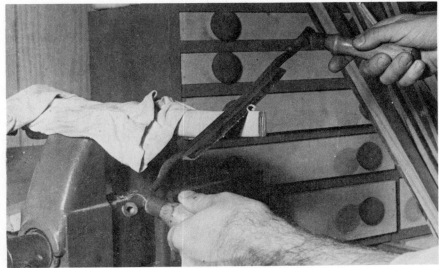

Often you will have to dress down the new handle a bit. An old-fashioned drawknife works well for this job. Note that the handle has been wrapped in rags to protect it from the vise jaws.

When the handle will fit the tool properly, drive it firmly into place. Then cut off the excess wood with a hacksaw.

The last step is to drive wedges in place and cut off any rough edges on the handle.

Axes and Mauls

These are repaired in the same manner as you would a hammer. Make sure you choose the proper handle for your particu-lar type of axe. There are a great number of sizes and lengths of axes, hatchets, and hammers available. A long thin wedge such as needed for an axe head can be made from a piece of hardwood such as oak; it does a better job of holding than several small steel wedges. You have to make a starting slot for the wedge with a large wood chisel. Then drive the wedge in as far as it will go and cut it off flush with the top of the axe head. Splitting mauls use a hollow round wedge to hold them securely in place. These are driven in place just the same as the flat wedges. Cutting the toe of the axe handle off flat will make it easier to drive the handle in place, and it won't upset the action of the axe.

Picks

Pick handles are installed in reverse. The small end of the handle is pushed down from the top of the pick and the handle driven in place as far into the pick head as possible, then the protruding handle portion is cut off flush with the top of the pick. No wedges are used because they would force the handle out of the top of the pick.

Some tools, such as this split-ting maul, use circular wedges.

Hayforks

Hayfork handles are fitted with a metal ferrule. Drive out the fork portion by tapping on the top of it. Then drive the new one up in the metal ferrule. Potato forks are repaired in the same manner.

Shovels

Basically, there are two types of shovel handles: solid wood, which are used on long-handled shovels, and combination wood and metal, which are used on short-handled shovels and spades.

To fit a handle to a long-handled shovel, the first step is to cut off the rivet head which runs through the metal ferrule on the shovel. Then drive out the rivet. (Use a cold chisel to slice off the rivet head.) This allows you to remove the broken portion which remains in the metal ferrule. Drive it out from the back side of the shovel. An old metal bolt works best for this job because it doesn't cut into the metal like a punch or chisel. Then fit the shaped wooden end into the metal ferrule. It may take a bit of final shaping and hammering to get it in properly. Bore a hole for a new rivet through the new handle. A 16-penny nail makes a great replacement rivet. Drive it in place, cut it off, leaving about $\frac{3}{16}$ of an inch protruding and peen (flatten) it down to make a "rivet head."

Short-handled shovels, which have a metal handle on the upper end, are fitted in the same manner. Make sure you get the handle fitted square with the shovel blade, not turned to one side.

Rehandling a shovel is easy. After sawing off the rivet head holding the handle in the shovel ferule, use a metal punch to drive out the rivet. Remove the old pieces of the shovel handle.

81

In a pinch, you can use a 16-penny nail for a rivet. Drive it in place in the bored hole, then cut it off and peen it over.

Rakes

Handles for heavy-duty rakes are fitted with a metal ferrule in one end. The better handles will be predrilled for the rake head tang. Tap out the old rake. (It's easier to place the rake in a vise and tap the old metal ferrule off with a heavy punch or chisel.) Then drive the rake tang up into the new handle ferrule. Other light-duty rakes are fitted with a metal ferrule. You repair them in the same manner as long-handle shovels. Remove the pin or rivet, remove the old wood and drive the new handle in the metal ferrule of the rake head. Then rivet with a nail.

Hoes

Hoe handles also come fitted with a metal ferrule. Again the tang of the tool is driven out of the old ferrule, then driven into the ferrule of the new handle. Some hoes may have a metal ferrule attached to the tang.

Pruning Shears

Long-handled pruning shears also have handles fitted into metal ferrules. Occasionally the handle will become loose in the ferrule. A combination of epoxy glue and wooden wedges driven down beside the metal tang will hold the handles securely in place.

Screwdrivers

You can make your own screwdriver, chisel and other small shop tool handles easily. Turn them out on a woodworking lathe, bore the hole and glue the metal tang in place with epoxy glue. Or you can use plastic handle-rods available from Brownell's Inc., Route 2, Box 1, Montezuma, Iowa 50171. Cut the plastic blanks to length with a hacksaw, then bore a slightly undersize hole in the handle. Heat the tool tang until it will melt the plastic then ram it down in the hole. The plastic will cool around the metal and hold it securely in place.

Knives

Kitchen knife handles are held in place by rivets. To make a replacement handle, cut a small hardwood blank for each side of the blade to the rough size of the blade. Clamp to the blade and bore rivet holes in both handle sides. Then rivet together using special rivets. Grind the handle down to fit the shape of the knife blade using a disc sander or belt sander. Polish smooth. Knife handles, blanks and rivets are available from Indian Ridge Traders, 306 South Washington, Royal Oak, Michigan 48068.

While you're installing new handles you might check the rest of the tool as well.

Rehandling a kitchen knife. Clamp the wooden handle blanks to the blade, bore for rivets, then place rivets together and tap down solidly. Grind the handles to fit the shape of the knife blade.

Steel brush off rust and give a light dust coating with a rust preventive oil such as WD-40. Or you might wish to spray the entire tool head with a new coat of paint. I paint all mine with fluorescent paint so they're easy to spot in the weeds. Give the handles a light oiling with linseed oil, wiping off excess oil before you finish.

Chapter 7

How to Use and Maintain Chain Saws

I grew up on a farm where there was one chore that was sure to keep us busy: wood cutting. My first experiences were with a big old double-bitted axe. We finally acquired a chain saw, a brute of a machine, and, to be truthful, I much preferred the axe. As far as I am concerned, the invention of the lightweight chain saw has been a blessing. Operating a chain saw is fun and easy, but there are two very important things to consider: safety and equipment maintenance. Because many chain saws are purchased by people who have never used them before, both the saws and the people sometimes suffer.

Just like any other tool, a chain saw must be treated respectfully, used safely, and maintained properly. Although chain saws are far from new to me, I have had a couple of minor accidents, and both could have been prevented with just plain common sense.

A couple of years ago I was felling a large tree. I watched closely for it to start to fall, and when it did I started to move back quickly away from the butt. I made two mistakes: I hadn't cleared the area of debris, and I didn't shut off the chain saw fast enough. I tripped and fell on the chain. The chain cut completely through a pair of

The development of the lightweight chainsaw has allowed the average person to cut firewood quickly and easily.

the saw is idling. If the chain moves while the saw is idling, you can get a nasty cut by falling on it, or brushing it against your body.

3. Never try to stop a moving chain with your hand. Never allow a moving chain to come in contact with your clothing.

4. Start your saw on a firm surface, the ground if possible.

5. Always turn off the saw before moving to make another cut.

6. Clear all debris away from area of cutting. This is especially important when felling a tree.

7. Watch out for falling limbs and bark. Wear a hard hat, heavy cap or hat.

8. Carefully examine tree that is to be felled or limbs to be removed to make sure they won't fall on power lines, buildings, etc.

heavy jeans; and I still have a nasty scar or my thigh. The second accident also could have been easily prevented. I was removing a large limb from one of our shade trees and it fell, knocking the ladder out from under me. I fell along with the chain saw, but luckily all I hurt was my dignity. If placed properly, the ladder might not have been hit by the limb.

Safety

As you can see, most chain saw accidents can be prevented easily by following a few safety rules:

1. Always make sure the chain is sharp. A dull chain causes you to put pressure on the saw and leaves you off guard should something happen.

2. Make sure the chain has the proper tension, and that the clutch is properly adjusted. The chain should not move while

Always clear away brush and debris from the area. A hard hat or other headgear will protect you from falling dead branches.

9. Keep children and pets away from cutting area.

10. Always refuel saw on bare ground in an area where there is nothing burnable. Prevent spilling fuel; move saw a few feet from fueling area before starting it.

11. Always make sure there is a clear exit from a falling tree and never stand directly behind a tree you're felling. The butt of the tree can kick back and up and kill you.

Don't let all these precautions scare you. If used properly, a chain saw can be a mighty valuable tool, and it can save you money.

Cutting Limbs

One of the most common uses of light-weight chain saws is pruning or removing unwanted tree limbs from a standing tree. Removing small limbs is not difficult, but a few extra precautions are needed for larger limbs. Place the ladder so you can easily reach the limb and so the falling limb can't knock the ladder out of place. You may wish to start the saw on the ground, tie a rope to it, and pull it up rather than trying to start it while up on a ladder. In any event, when working on large limbs and those high off the ground, it's a good idea to secure yourself to the tree with a safety rope. You may even wish to tie the saw to the tree with a short rope so it can't be dropped to the ground.

When pruning large limbs, make an undercut on the limb about two to three feet from the trunk. Then cut through from top of the limb to allow it to fall. Make a third cut, another undercut next to the trunk, and follow with a fourth cut from top to remove the stub. If only one or two cuts are used, the weight of the falling limb will break off portions of the trunk and bark on the underside. Normally, on smaller limbs,

Make the first cut a short distance out from the trunk, at the underside of the limb. Work gloves and safety goggles are always a good idea.

After cutting off the main portion from the top, remove the stub the same way, starting from the underside.

only three cuts are needed. Cut away the limb leaving stub, then cut the stub off directly down from the top.

It's a good idea to paint the cut area with tree-wound dressing, or even latex paint to prevent disease and insect infestation.

When removing extremely small limbs, make sure the chain is running before touching it to limb. Otherwise, a whippy limb can stop the chain and jerk you off balance.

Firewood

A second common use of chain saws is cutting firewood. People all over the country are learning how to cut costs by cutting their own firewood for fireplaces and old-fashioned woodstoves. It's not necessary to own your own woodlands to do this. Firewood may be cut and removed from many public lands—national forests, state forests, even county and city woodlands, *providing you obtain permission from the proper agency.* When the cost of a cord of firewood (128 cubic feet) exceeds $100 as it usually does in the cities, the benefits of cutting your own firewood are readily apparent.

The best time of the year to cut firewood is in the early spring when damaged trees and branches are left from winter storms. Wood cut at this time will dry by fall and burn properly. When cutting firewood anywhere, but especially in national forests and public lands, make sure the chain saw is equipped with spark-arresting muffler screens.

Most often you can get all the firewood you'll need from deadfalls, or trees blown down by winter storms, but sometimes you have to resort to felling a tree. Although felling a tree sounds complicated and extremely dangerous, it is neither if you follow safety rules and use good common sense.

FOLLOW THESE STEPS. Carefully examine the area around the tree to make sure the falling tree won't damage property; and keep other people and pets out of the area.

To make the tree fall in the direction you wish, you will have to first make an undercut notch. Unless the tree is leaning too far in the wrong direction, it will normally fall in the direction of the removed notch. Make the notch about one-third the thickness of the tree as shown. Then cut from the back of the tree toward the notch and about two inches above center of notch. Don't cut all the way through, but leave a bit of wood between the notch and the final back cut. This acts as a hinge and helps prevent the tree butt from jumping up in the air.

In tree felling, cut a notch on the side you want the tree to fall.

The last cut is from the back of tree to the notch, leaving a "hinge" between the cuts.

As soon as the tree starts to fall, shut off the saw, set it down and get away from the area as quickly as possible. If there is any kind of brush or debris around the tree, make sure you clear it away before felling the tree.

After felling, your next step is to "limb" the tree or remove the limbs. Always cut so the tree won't sag and pinch or bind the saw chain, and always stand on the uphill side of a tree when cutting on sloping ground. Otherwise, when a limb is released, the tree may roll over on you.

After removing all limbs, the third step is to "buck" or cut the log into the proper lengths. Again stand uphill of the log if on sloping ground. On smaller trees and logs, you should place the log over something to raise it and to help avoid digging the chain into the ground. When a chain saw hits the ground, it loses its sharpness in seconds. If you're cutting a supported log, first make a top cut about a third of the way through, then cut from the bottom to allow the log to fall.

If you're cutting a large log into lengths for firewood, cut all lengths almost all the way through, but don't allow the chain to go completely through and into the ground. Then, using a heavy bar, roll the log over and complete the cuts.

After cutting logs into lengths, you'll probably want to split them to provide better burning fireplace wood. Splitting is an old-time job that requires little knowledge, but a strong back and lots of work. It will sure tone up those muscles. Don't try to split woods such as elm; you'll only end up saying words you thought you'd forgotten.

Wood splits much easier as soon as it is cut, rather than after is has cured. By using a special splitting maul, you can also make the job easier. This is a heavy, wide-angled axe that provides the weight and leverage needed for splitting logs.

Clear the area of people, take a firm stance, make sure there is nothing overhead or behind you, look directly at where you aim to strike, and swing with force. If you look carefully at the end of the wood chunk before starting to split it, you'll notice how the grain runs. Splitting with the grain is much easier than against it.

Maintenance

A simple check-up before using a chain saw can not only prevent serious problems from developing but keep the tool running and cutting smoothly. There are just six basic steps to keeping a chain saw in good shape, and they take only a few moments before heading for the woods and starting up:

1. Wipe all accumulated oil and sawdust from the chain saw housing. A chain saw really gets dirty, and accumulations of dirt, sawdust and oil eventually clog oiler holes and air filters.

2. Remove the air breather filter from the carburator and shake off any accumulated dust. If the filter is really dirty, take it *outside* and clean it in a can of gasoline.

3. Remove the cover plate from the clutch and clean out all accumulated dirt, especially around the oiler passages and the chain tension screw.

4. Make sure the chain tension is correct. Hold the chain bar up with one hand and adjust the tension screw so the chain moves freely, but doesn't sag.

5. Make sure the bolts holding the chain bar in place are tight. If loose, the chain sags, causing undue wear on the bar and chain; and it's downright dangerous.

6. Fill the chain oiler with the proper oil and fill the fuel tank with the proper fuel mixture.

FUEL MIXTURES. When oil is mixed with gasoline to make up the two-cycle fuel mixture it is not enough to pour in the specified amount of oil and the specified amount of gasoline. The ingredients must be mixed thoroughly.

If gasoline and oil are not mixed thoroughly, varying gasoline-to-oil mixtures will eventually be put in the fuel tank. If fuel is not properly mixed, it's possible to have mixtures that vary from 10 to 1 to 100 to 1 even though the correct quantities for a 40 to 1 mix were poured into a container.

Improper mixtures can create operating problems that might be mistakenly blamed on carburetion or ignition.

To mix fuel properly, pour half the desired amount of gasoline (one gallon if filling a two-gallon container) into a fuel container. The container should be equipped with a strainer and a flexible spout for easy pouring.

Pour the measured amount of oil into the gasoline and mix this thoroughly for four minutes. When the time has elapsed, pour in the remaining quantity of gasoline and continue to mix for another three minutes. If mixed in this manner, there's a good chance the oil and gasoline will remain mixed. Fuel containers should probably be reshaken each time before fuel is poured into a tank.

Use regular grade gasoline, preferably one that is low in lead content. High octane, leaded gasolines are not satisfactory. Deposits that can accumulate from leaded fuels can cause spark plug problems and piston burning.

Refineries formulate fuel differently for winter and summer use. In the winter, additives are added to fight water accumulation and to make gasoline more volatile. If this fuel is used in the summer or when weather warms up, the fuel boils quickly, vapors expand in the fuel lines and vapor locks occur.

Summer gasolines are formulated to slow down the vaporization and to allow fuel to get into the combustion chamber before it vaporizes into a combustible form.

Some additives blended into gasolines can separate or be isolated as a result of incomplete combustion or if the fuel is permitted to stand a long time. These additives create varnish-like deposits that can cause carburetor needles to stick, and may cause conductive-type deposits to form on spark plugs. It is best not to store fuel mixture for more than three or four months.

Sharpening

There is nothing more frustrating than a chain saw that won't cut. A dull chain won't cut hot butter while a sharp chain

If your chain is slightly dull, you can touch it up quickly with a chain saw file. Or, if you're new at using chainsaws, try a sharpening guide as shown on pages 90-91.

will whiz right through the toughest piece of oak. A saw chain should be kept sharp at all times, and, although you can have it sharpened by a professional, it's easy to do yourself, and even easier to keep it sharp.

SHARPENING GUIDES. Although a saw chain can be touched up by hand without using a guide, it's not recommended for the inexperienced to attempt to sharpen a dull chain without one. Without a guide, one side of the chain inevitably ends up a bit sharper than the other, or, if the sharpening angles differ, the chain wanders and the chain bar binds.

There are several chain saw sharpening guides on the market costing from about $2 to $20. I have one of the more expensive guides because, with 85 acres of timber, we cut a lot of wood for our fireplaces and old wood stove and it takes constant sharpening to keep my chain saws in good shape.

The chain sharpener shown is one of the easiest units to use I have found. It's adjustable to any tooth angle or depth, so you can sharpen an old worn chain as readily as a newer one.

USING THE GUIDE. The first step in using the unit shown is to clamp it to the bar. A small clamp on the top of the unit is screwed down on the chain to hold it in place and prevent it from chattering. The chain should still be allowed to turn freely. The back of the chain tooth is held against a spring metal pawl. Adjust the file holder to sharpen the tooth at the proper sharpening angle as specified by your chain manufacturer. A spring-loaded screw on the front of the unit is set allowing the file to sharpen only so far. This enables you to sharpen all teeth the same amount. Different sizes of files can be used in the unit, and make sure the file used is the correct size for the chain teeth on your unit.

With the unit properly adjusted, stroke across the chain tooth, cutting with the file only on the stroke.

Turn chain to the next tooth on the same side of the chain and sharpen it. After sharpening all teeth on one side, loosen the wing nut on top of the unit and swing the file to sharpen the teeth on the opposite side.

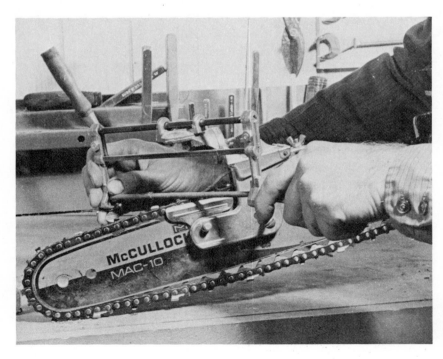

An adjustable sharpening guide such as this makes it easy to sharpen a chain without removing it from the saw.

90

Fasten the guide to the chainsaw bar; then clamp the chain so that it turns smoothly but doesn't chatter or move with the file.

Use the screw on top to adjust the depth of the cut. This screw insures that the sharpening depth is the same for all teeth.

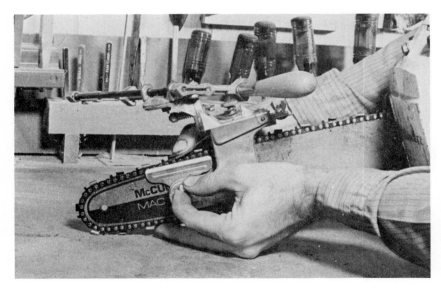

The guide holds each tooth in place while you stroke against the tooth. After filing all the teeth on one side, turn the guide unit to the same angle to sharpen teeth on the other side.

DEPTH GAUGE. The speed at which a chain saw cuts is governed by the depth gauge. If your saw is throwing out fine sawdust and cuts slow, the depth gauges should be jointed down. The wood chips should be fairly large and even shaped. The depth gauges should be filed down a bit each time you sharpen the chain, because each time you sharpen the chain the teeth become lower. These can be cut down with a couple of strokes of the file on the adjustable unit, or you can use a simpler hand-held depth gauge jointer to guide the file and cut the gauges to the correct depth.

Keeping your chain saw sharp is not only necessary for an easy-working saw, but for safety as well.

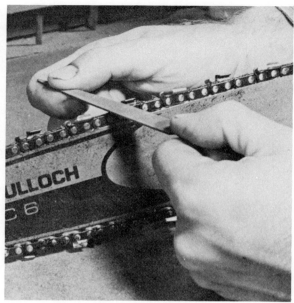

Each time you sharpen the chain, lower the depth gauges by filing them slightly.

Chapter 8

Repairing Lawn Mowers

Everyone knows a hard-driven power mower should be serviced before winter storage. However, few of us manage this easy task and, as a result, we end up with a hard-to-start and cranky power mower come springtime. Or, sometimes, even if we can get it started, it becomes increasingly more difficult to get the machine going. In either case, now's the time to give it a complete maintenance job. Unless your mower has been frequently neglected, or has severe mechanical problems, a weekend spent cleaning, retightening and readjusting will usually assure an easy spring start. The job is not complicated and requires only a screwdriver, pliers, a small socket set and a small open-end wrench set.

Remove Engine

The first job is to separate the engine from the mower housing. This enables you to clean the housing completely, as well as work on a workbench. Removing the engine from a two-cycle mower is simple; remove the spark plug wire (to prevent accidental starting), take off the blade, loosen a few bolts and lift the engine off. On a four-cycle mower, the problem is complicated by the crankcase. On most mowers, you also have to remove the blade holder

By detatching the engine, you can clean and tune up the entire mower most easily.

from the crankshaft to enable the engine to be removed. The blade holder is held in place on the shaft by a combination of a bolt and a woodruff key. Lightly rapping the holder with a small hammer will usually work the holder off the shaft. Don't lose the tiny key.

Clean Underside of Housing

With the engine separated from the housing, you can easily remove the handle, wheels, and any mechanical controls such as the throttles and choke. Turn the housing upside down and scrape off the worst of the grass clippings and rust using a paint scraper and large screwdriver no longer useful for driving screws. Follow this with a stiff wire brush to clean off remaining rust.

To prevent rusting of the housing, spray it with either a rust preventive oil, or a good rust-inhibiting (not resistant) paint. Using a soft cloth and kerosene (not quite as dangerous as gasoline), wipe the entire housing down to remove any oil, grease or dirt. Touch up any chipped paint or rust-

Next, go over the underside of the housing with a steel brush to remove all the stubborn rust.

ing areas or spray the entire housing with a good rust-inhibiting paint.

Replace the handle, place a smear of grease on the wheel bolts and fasten the wheels back in place. Make sure you have the mower set at the proper cutting height, determined by the bolt holes the wheels are fastened in. (On some models this may be determined by the number of washers on the blade shaft.) Some self-propelled mowers have a rubber gear that supplies power to the rear wheels. These gears become worn in a couple of seasons and should be replaced.

Clean Engine

Set the mower housing aside and begin work on the engine. Be sure the spark plug wire has been removed. Using solvent, soft cloths and a small stiff bristle brush, wash, scrub, and wipe the engine clean, making sure you get down into the smallest areas. Don't forget the cooling fins, as clogged fins can decrease engine performance greatly. On some engines you may have to remove the sheet metal covers to get at the fins. Remove cowlings as necessary.

One very important but frequently forgotten detail, especially with two-cycle engines, is to carefully remove the muffler and scrape off any carbon deposits that may be surrounding the ports or blocking the muffler. Be careful not to drop any particles down into the cylinder. It's a good idea to turn the piston up so it will close the cylinder off. Replace the muffler and gasket.

If your mower has a rewind starter with a built-in rope, pull the starter rope out slowly to its full length and examine it for any cuts or abrasions. If your mower has a mechanical rewind starter, examine it for loose or missing parts, and lubricate according to your owner's manual. Inspect the nut on the flywheel and tighten if necessary.

Clean Fuel Tank

Remove the fuel tank and line. Put about a cup or two of lacquer thinner in the fuel tank, drop in a handful of small pebbles and shake the tank thoroughly to break up all the old gum and varnish. Pour this out and rinse the tank with clean gasoline.

Remove the muffler and clean it and the exhaust ports of carbon. This is especially important in 2-cycle engines.

Remove cowlings, gas tank, and other items so that all areas can be thoroughly cleaned.

Adjust Carburetor and Air Filter

Adjust the carburetor to the initial setting as per your owner's manual. It may have vibrated out of adjustment over the past summer. Remove the air filter cover and filter. Place the filter in gasoline (outside) and let it sit for a bit. Remove it and scrub thoroughly with a good stiff brush, then place it back in the sun to dry thoroughly. Clean out the area around the filter with small cotton swabs. Some mowers have replaceable paper air filters; in this case, insert a new filter of the type recommended by the manufacturer.

If your mower has a sediment bowl trap and fuel filter, remove the filter and clean it as above. Dump the water and sediment out and replace the filter and bowl. If you're in doubt about the fuel lines, either blow through them or replace them.

Bolt the engine back on the housing and fasten on the blade holder making sure the key fits the slot.

Place the end of the spark plug wire about $\frac{1}{16}$ of an inch away from the housing and turn the engine over by hand. If a healthy blue spark jumps across the gap, the ignition is working properly. If the spark is yellow or weak, the ignition system should be serviced before the season starts.

Check Spark Plug

Remove the spark plug and examine it carefully. The condition it's in will give you a good idea how your machine is functioning. If the tip of the insulator is a light grey or tan with very little combustion deposits, the engine is operating normally. Clean the plug with fine emery cloth, regap it according to your owner's manual and replace. However, if the plug is worn out it will be whitish and slightly eroded, and should be replaced with a new plug, gapped according to your manual. An overheated plug will be white and burned. Usually, this is caused by either a too-lean carburetor setting, air leak or obstruction in the fuel line, a loose carburetor mounting, or a ruptured fuel diaphram. On two-cycle engines, it can also mean a clogged muffler or exhaust ports. If the electrode on the spark plug has built up a heavy deposit reaching between electrodes, there is too much carbon in the cylinder. With two-cycle engines, it means improper fuel-oil mixture or clogged exhaust ports.

Inspect and clean the carburetor. Clean the air filter and filter housing, and if the gasket is loose, replace it.

If the end of the plug is wet, dark and slightly oily, it could mean an overfilled crankcase on a four-cycle engine, or possibly a worn oil-control ring. On a two-cycle engine it indicates excessive oil or use of nonrecommended oil in fuel. The idle speed may be too low or the idle adjustment too rich, or it may be simply a clogged air filter.

Check all nuts, bolts and screws and tighten any that are loose. Spray a light dusting coat of penetrating, rust inhibiting oil into hard to reach areas and lubricate any fittings.

Sharpen Mower Blade

If your mower blade is in pretty fair shape, you can easily sharpen it with a good mill bastard file, single cut. Place the blade in a vise and file the edges, keeping the correct angle and not "rounding off" the blade. You should keep the blade as balanced as possible; to do this, use the balancing gadget mentioned in Chapter 4 (p. 57).

If your blade is in bad shape with deep nicks in the edges, you may need to grind the edge with a power grinder. Be careful to keep from overheating the edge and ruining the temper of the metal or you will have an edge that will do nothing but "fold over" the first time you use it.

Place the blade back on the mower (after again ensuring that spark plug wire is disconnected) and fill the tank with the proper fuel, or fuel and oil mixture. Inspect the entire machine to make sure everything is hooked up or replaced. Remove the spark plug and place a teaspoon of fuel into the cylinder, replace the spark plug and crank it up. The gasoline in the cylinder should cause the engine to fire on the first or second pull, and the piston will then pump the gasoline into the carburetor and keep the motor running. It will probably be running a bit rough and the

carburetor settings should be carefully adjusted according to your owner's manual.

Riding Lawnmowers and Small Garden Tractors

In addition to the regular maintenance done on push mowers, riding mowers and small garden tractors require additional work.

One of the first jobs is to inspect and adjust the brakes and clutch as needed. This should be done periodically throughout the season. Make sure the brake and clutch will stop the mower operating at full speed, and that any auxiliary or parking brakes will hold the mower on a slope. The spindle brake on the blade must stop the blade within seconds.

Check the clutch and brakes on riding mowers.

97

Inspect all drive belts, chains, gear boxes and so on and lubricate or tighten them as needed.

Inspect and adjust all belt and chain tensions. Chain tension should be about ¼-inch slack for most units, but check the manufacturer's instructions for your machine.

Carefully examine the deck to make sure no bolts or fasteners have worked loose.

On mowers that may be stood on end for storage, make sure you remove the battery before you stand them on end. Batteries should be stored on wooden supports up off a concrete floor.

Lubricate the machine according to the manufacturer's instructions, paying particular attention to such places as a chain case, axle bearings and differential.

Chapter 9

Tillers and Snowthrowers

Tiller Maintenance

With today's soaring food prices, more and more people are growing their own fruit and vegetables. One of the gardener's great helpmates is the rotary tiller. A power tiller is a fine piece of equipment that can not only save you time and effort, but money as well. A tiller is much like a lawn mower, and it should be maintained regularly and properly. As is the case of most equipment, the engine requires the most maintenance.

Preventive maintenance can prolong the life of your tiller and keep it working efficiently. Always use fresh clean gasoline, regular or low-lead type. Old gasoline creates gums and varnishes that eventually stick carburetor parts. Old gasoline also won't vaporize properly for a good fuel-air mixture.

Watch your tiller tines carefully. If they become entangled with old twine, heavy roots or other materials, stop the engine and remove the material before it bogs down the tiller and causes the engine to overwork. Replace any broken tines.

It's a good idea to give your tiller a quick "inspection" each time before you use it. These are some maintenance tips suggested by a leading tiller manufacturer:

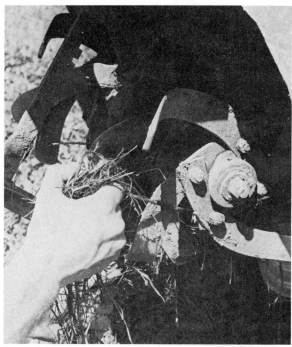

Keeping the tines free of tangling debris is an important part of tiller maintenance.

1. *Make sure the transmission has 90 or 140 weight gear oil.* Regularly check the gear oil level and make sure the oil is to the full line. Constantly check your tiller for evidence of oil leaks at wheel shaft, tiller shaft, front of drive shaft, and rear of drive shaft.

Check the oil level frequently.

2. Probably the single most important maintenance job is to *check the engine oil level.* Check the engine oil level every two hours during continuous operation. I always make it a point also to check the oil dipstick before each tilling job.

3. *Always use new SE or SD No. 30 weight oil, or old MS rated oil.* Keep the oil level up *close to the "full" mark* at all times. The oil in your tiller should be drained and replaced with fresh *new oil at about every 10 hours.* If your garden is extremely dusty, you'll probably want to change oil sooner.

4. *Remove and clean the air cleaner* every 10 hours, or more often if tilling conditions are extremely dusty. Your engine may have one of three types of air cleaners: sponge, oil bath or paper and each should be checked and cleaned according to the manufacturer's instructions.

5. One very important job is to *check the engine cooling fins* frequently. They must be kept clean and clear of debris to allow the engine to cool properly.

6. Use the "oil-can treatment" frequently; *oil all moving parts* such as shift linkages, yoke pivot points, depth adjustment bar and lockpin and wheel shafts (for easy wheel removal when necessary).

7. *Check and tighten nuts and bolts. Replace* any that are missing.

8. *Check the tension of the belts* regularly to assure a ⅜-inch deflection. Replace any overstretched, broken, badly worn or very "shiny" (evidence of slippage) belts with the proper belts. It is important for proper adjustments of forward, as well as pulley and reverse disc alignment to have properly fitting belts.

9. *Check adjustment of reverse spring* to make sure it "pops" tiller out of reverse gear when the clutch lever is released. Adjust reverse adjustment bolt upward until it functions properly.

Oil linkages and pivot points often.

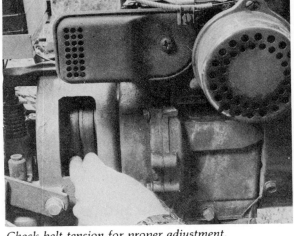

Check belt tension for proper adjustment.

Properly tighten all adjustment nuts and bolts.

Make sure the forward-reverse adjustment is right.

10. *Remove and check spark plug.* A spark plug from an engine can tell you whether your engine is operating properly, or, if not, what the trouble may be. If the spark plug is evenly colored and light tan or grey all over, it and the engine are working properly. Replace the spark plug once a year.

If the engine is overheating, the spark plug electrode will have a white, dusty blistered look. A good reason might be the cooling fins are plugged, or the carburetor is set too lean. If the spark plug is damp and oily, or coated with a dark substance, the carburetor may be set with too rich a mixture.

Use a socket wrench to remove and check spark plug.

Winterizing Your Tiller

When fall rolls around and it's time to put your tiller up for winter storage, it should be given a thorough inspection and maintenance with special attention to several details.

1. *Drain all the gasoline from the engine.* Leave just enough gas in the tank to run the engine for a few minutes to heat up the engine and burn out any remaining gas. Pour a tablespoon of clean engine oil in the tank to prevent it from rusting.

2. While the engine is hot, *drain the engine oil and refill* the crankcase with new 30-weight detergent oil.

3. *Remove the spark plug* and *pour a tablespoon of clean engine oil in the spark plug hole.* Then turn engine over by slowly pulling on starter rope. This distributes oil in the top of the cylinder and prevents rusting.

4. *Remove the air cleaner and clean or replace as necessary.*

5. If your tiller has an electric starter, *disconnect the battery* and place on a board or other insulator. Check the battery once a month for acid level and corrosion of posts. Wash any corroded posts with a bit of baking soda and water. Don't store your battery on a concrete floor or metal surface as these materials may drain the electricity from the battery.

6. *Lubricate all moving parts.*

7. *Check transmission oil; fill up to the level line.*

Snowthrower Maintenance

Like all other machinery, snow removal equipment does its best if given periodic inspections and preventive maintenance before bad trouble starts. The job won't take more than an hour or so. For tools, you need a set of small open-end wrenches, a grease gun, squirt oil can, screwdriver, a spark plug wrench (to fit plug), and spark plug gauge.

In maintaining snowthrowers, remember they are designed to operate most efficiently in wet winter conditions, as opposed to lawn mowers, which are operated in hot dusty weather. This means they are maintained differently. For instance, most snow throwers don't have air filters over the carburetor, but are fitted with guards or shields to keep moisture away from the carburetor and other parts of the engine.

CHECK THE OIL. The first step is to wheel the machine out in the open where you can easily work around it. Start engine first; warm oil drains faster and sludge will be mixed rather than settled on crankcase bottom. Remove the oil drain plug in the crankcase and drain out all the old oil. Remove the oil filter cap and refill with the oil recommended by the manufacturer of the unit. In most cases, oil for winter use should be a high quality detergent oil classified for service SC, SD, or MS. Detergent oils keep the engine cleaner and help retard the formation of gum and varnish

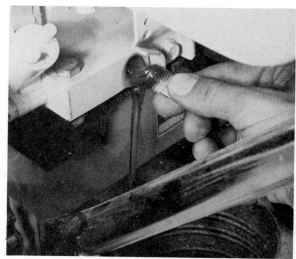

The old oil drains out better if it's warm. Run the snowthrower for a few minutes first.

102

Remove the oil filter cap and refill with proper weight oil.

deposits. For temperatures under 40 degrees Fahrenheit use SAE 5W-20, SAE 5W-30, SAE 10W, or SAE 10W-30. For temperatures below zero degrees Fahrenheit use SAE 10W or SAE 10W-30 diluted 10 per cent with kerosene. Use no other additives in the oil. Check the oil regularly, at least after each five hours of operation and keep the oil level up to the full point.

If your unit is equipped with a gear reduction drive, remove drain hole and drain out all of the old oil. It's best to do this after running gear train oil because gear oil is thick when cold. Fill with oil recommended by manufacturer. After about every 100 hours of engine operation, remove the bottom drain plug and check the oil level of the gear box.

CHECK SPARK PLUG. Using the proper size wrench, remove the spark plug and examine it closely. Your spark plug is a good indicator of how your engine is operating. If the insulator on the plug is a light tan or gray color, the engine is operating normally. Depending on whether your engine is a two cycle or four cycle, the spark plug may indicate different en-

gine problems. On a two-cycle engine a white blistered electrode indicates that the carburetor is possibly set too lean, the engine is overloading, or something is blocking the engine cooling fins. If the plug is wet, black and oil fouled, it may indicate a too-rich carburetor setting or the wrong fuel-oil mix. On a four-cycle engine a blistered plug also means engine overheating or a too lean carburetor mixture. A wet, fouled plug may indicate worn valve guides, oil rings, or a plugged breather.

In any case, after examining your plug and diagnosing any problems, clean and reset the gap according to the manufacturer's instructions. Use a spark plug feeler gauge of the correct thickness, and don't guess at the gap opening or use the old "dime" trick. The spark plug should be cleaned and regapped after every 100 hours of operation. The best method of cleaning is to scrape or wire brush and wash with gasoline. (Caution: Do this out in the open, not in an enclosed area.) If plug is worn out, replace with a new plug set according to manufacturer's instructions.

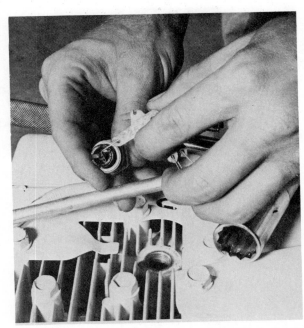
With spark plug wrench, remove plug. Check it, and clean and regap it to the manufacturer's specifications.

STARTING EQUIPMENT. If the engine on your unit is a manual start, gently pull out the starter rope and examine it for any frayed spots. If the unit is an electric start with battery, refill with water and make sure battery is fully charged. (Do this with battery disconnected from motor to prevent damaging starter motor.) If your unit has one of the new AC plug-in starters, check to ensure there are no breaks or worn insulated spots on cord, that the prongs aren't bent out of shape and that the cord grounding lead is well grounded.

BLADES. Of course, one of the most abused areas of snowthrowers is the rotating snow pick-up blades. These should be inspected carefully to make sure none of the blades are broken, cracked or could come apart and cause harm to the machine or operator. On most units, the front pick-up blade rotates on an axle with bearings at either end. These bearings must be kept lubricated using a good automotive grease. The grease fitting may be on the ends or in the middle of the shaft, depending on your machine.

LUBRICATE PARTS. The drive chain sprocket on some units will also be fitted with a grease fitting and this should be given a bit of grease as well. In greasing wintertime machines, use a light grade of grease such as Citgo TORJAN HMA-1 or its equivalent to ensure easy working of the parts.

Place a few drops of lightweight oil such as 10W-30 on all remaining drive sprocket bushings, axle bushings, auger drive chain, rear wheel drive-chain and throttle, gear shift and governor linkages.

WHEELS. The wheels are held on most units by a small pin driven through the wheel hub flange and into the axle. Check to make sure the pins haven't worked out and the wheels are secure. If tires are inflatable, make sure tire pressure is up.

CHAIN. Remove chain guard covers and check for chain tension, as well as any possible chain flaws. If chain is badly worn, broken, or needs replacement, replace using a new chain-repair link. The normal chain tension on most units should allow between ⅛- and ¼-inch deflection.

Snowthrower blades are fitted on a bearing shaft. Keep it lubricated with automotive grease.

An oil squirt can will help to oil chains or sprocket drives.

Wheel-securing pins can sometimes work loose and fall out, as this one has. Check to be sure the pin is there.

NUTS, BOLTS, SCREWS. Snowthrowers, like most outdoor power equipment, are subject to a lot of vibration, and one of the most important chores is to ensure that all nuts, bolts and screws are tight and secure. This is especially important around the chain guards, snow deflection chute and engine mounting bolts.

CONTROLS. Check all controls, throttle, shifting mechanism, etc., and make sure that all nuts, bolts and screws are tight and secure. This is especially important around the chain guards, snow deflection chute and engine mounting bolts.

GASOLINE. Before starting engine, fill with clean, fresh, regular gasoline. Use a winter gasoline as it has a higher volatility which improves starting in cold weather. Do not use gasoline left over from summer lawn chores. If your engine is a two-cycle, mix oil and fuel mixture properly in a can, shake well, then pour into another can marked for your snowthrower. Fill tank from that can only.

OTHER TIPS. In addition to a good preventive check, there are things you can do that will not only assist your unit to operate more efficiently, but prolong its life as well. After using the snowthrower, continue to run it for about 10 minutes in an area free of snow. This gives the engine an opportunity to "burn off" some of the moisture that it might have collected. (Caution: Do this only in a well-ventilated area to prevent possible poisoning from carbon monoxide fumes.)

105

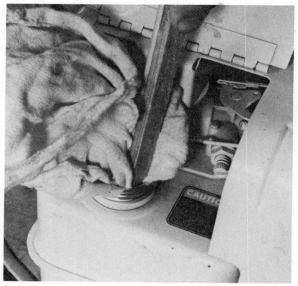

For off-season storage, drain the gas tank and dry it with a rag to prevent gum deposits.

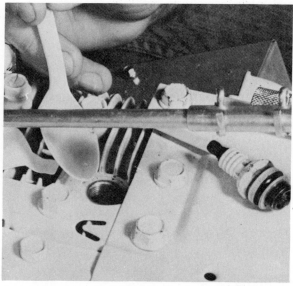

Just a teaspoon of oil is all that's needed after changing crankcase oil. Crank the engine over by hand to distribute it evenly.

It is a good idea to "dust spray" the inside of the blade housing and chute with a good rust preventive such as WD-40 after each use. Do not run your snowthrower for any length of time during hot weather, as you may cause overheating of engine due to shielding on the engine for wet weather.

After the season is over, a few preventive maintenance tips can also help ensure a well-operating, fast-starting machine for next season. The first step is to drain all fuel from the tank and swab it dry with a clean absorbent rag. This prevents gum deposits from forming in carburetor, fuel lines and tank.

While the engine is still warm, drain the oil from the crankcase and refill with fresh oil.

Remove the spark plug, pour in a teaspoon of oil and crank engine over slowly by hand to distribute the oil. Replace the spark plug. Regrease and oil all parts and dust spray entire unit with WD-40 to protect from rusting. Place the unit in an out-of-the way, dust-free area until the next season. If unit has battery for electric start, remove battery and place it on a couple of boards. A battery placed directly on the concrete floor will soon be drained of energy.

With your snowthrower in tip-top shape you can wait for that big snowfall with assurance that you can clear your driveway and walks easily and quickly.

Chapter 10   Ladders

If you're a homeowner, sooner or later you'll need a ladder. Depending on what type you choose and how you use it, a ladder can be one of your best tools, or one of the most dangerous. As with any tool, quality is important. When your life depends on it, a good-quality ladder can more than pay for the extra money spent on it.

There are many different kinds of ladders, but there are basically three grades: *household* (which is the cheaper kind), *commercial* and *industrial.* For most home chores, a commercial-grade ladder would be well suited. You also have the choice of wood, aluminum, or even fiberglass. Although each has advantages and disadvantages, the choice is mostly personal unless you will be doing quite a bit of electrical work; then a non-conductive wooden or fiberglass ladder would be necessary. Wooden ladders require a bit more care and are naturally heavier than those made of fiberglass or aluminum.

In selecting the ladder for your house or farm, remember that an extension ladder should be long enough so that three feet protrudes above the eaves, and should also include a three-rung overlap on the ladder. (When extended, the three bottom rungs of the extension must overlap with the three top rungs of the ladder.) If you know the height of your house or barn eaves, you can select the proper length ladder.

In most cases, you'll probably need more than one ladder, and an extension

For electrical work, use a wooden or fiberglass ladder.

Using the correct size ladder for the job will keep you safer—and speed up your work.

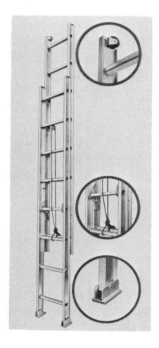

Basic features of a good extension ladder. Make sure the rope and pulley system is in good shape.

for use outside your house and out-buildings. One or two smaller step-ladders for light work around the house may also be necessary. Again, select the right size. Don't place a ladder on anything such as a table to add needed height.

Setting It Up

To set up an extension ladder properly, first place the bottom against the house foundation, then "walk" the ladder up rung by rung until it is leaning against the house. Then lift the ladder and pull it a couple of feet away from the house foundation. Grasp the extension rope and pull it to extend the ladder into the position you desire. Then again lift the bottom of the ladder and set it in place with the bottom distance from the house foundation to the ladder bottom no less than one-quarter the height of the ladder.

Make sure the ladder bottom is sitting squarely and securely in place. Don't prop up one leg with a rock or stick. If the ladder is sitting on a slick surface such as a concrete patio, place a couple of heavy objects such as concrete blocks against the legs to make sure that they won't slide. The top ends of the ladder should also be securely placed against the side of the house, or the eave. If the ladder is to be used for access to the roof, make sure it extends above the eave by at least three feet. Also make sure the extension overlap is at least three feet. If you need to move the ladder over a couple of feet, such as in painting, pull the top out and slide it over, then lift the bottom and move it over as well. Before you climb up on the ladder, make sure the locks are securely hooked, and that the extension rope is out of the way on the back of the ladder.

Avoid the two errors shown here: poor positioning of the ladder and overreaching.

Set up a ladder by placing the bottom against the house and "walking" it up rung by rung.

For safety, a ladder should be extended to reach three feet above the edge of the roof.

109

Using Ladders

Always climb facing the ladder and never go above the third rung from the top of the ladder. Stand squarely on the ladder with your body between the side rails and both feet on the rungs. Never lean out away from a ladder with one foot waving in the air for balance. Never stand on the top rung of a step ladder or on the paint tray, and make sure there is no dirt, paint, grease, or debris on the rungs. Always inspect the ladder before climbing up on it to make sure there are no broken or loose rungs.

Tempting, but wrong. Never stand on the paint tray of a step ladder—it isn't built to hold you.

Step Ladders

Setting up a step ladder correctly is also important. Either lean it against an object or open it up. Make sure it is fully opened if used in this manner, that the lock is down and secure, and that all four legs sit solidly on a level surface so the ladder doesn't tip or rock. Occasionally check the back cross-braces on step ladders to make sure they haven't cracked or loosened.

Accessories

In some instances, specialized ladder accessories such as *ladder jacks* may be needed. Often these can be rented from tool rental places. And some building suppliers will provide them if you buy a large amount of roofing material, windows, or other materials.

Ladder jacks are used with two ladders. You can either borrow a second ladder, or, if the height is right, separate your extension ladder and use the two halves. The ladder jacks are hooked over the ladder rungs and a scaffolding board is placed across between them resting on the cross supports. Use a good solid heavy board, or preferably a scaffolding board. The board should extend at least a couple of feet past the ladder jacks.

MAINTENANCE. A good ladder will last a lifetime if kept properly. It should be hung on a wall with large hooks or stored on edge.

Aluminum ladders need almost no upkeep, but wooden ladders occasionally need a coating of linseed oil for protection.

Never paint a wooden ladder; the paint may conceal a crack or break.

Chapter 11   Tire Repair

One of the first problems you encounter when you get to the farm is flat tires. Sharp rocks, old discarded nails, and thorns abound from one end of the country to another and, once you get off the beaten path, you might as well figure on having flats. In fact, I expect a flat on my old tractor about once every week or so, and, if I don't have one, I feel I'm not working hard enough!

Tubeless Tires

Most older farm equipment has tires with tubes; however newer equipment and most items such as tillers have tubeless tires. Tubeless tire flats can be repaired easily. Use a tubeless-tire repair kit and patch the tire right on the equipment. These kits include the tools, cement and plugs needed to patch a small puncture hole. Large holes must be repaired after removing the tire from the rim.

First locate the puncturing item and remove it. This may necessitate airing the tire up a bit if it is completely flat. The kit comes with a metal probe that can be used to help locate and dig out such items as nails. After removing the item from the hole, dip the probe in the cement and then push it into the puncture hole and lubricate the entire hole with the cement.

A second tool in the kit is a large needle with a slotted hole in it. Pieces of patching rubber strip are placed in the eye of the

A portable air tank is a great help. You can fill it up at home or at a service station and carry enough air to fill a tire or two right into the field.

needle, the backing paper is peeled away, then the entire rubber strip is dipped in cement and pushed into the hole. The needle is inserted all the way to the handle, then twisted a bit and pulled back out. The rubber strip stays in the hole and excess rubber from the strip is then cut off flush with the tire surface and that's all there is to it.

Removing Tires

In most cases, however, you will have to deal with tubes and this means removing the wheel from the equipment, then the tire from the wheel rim.

To patch a tubeless tire, remove the puncturing item. Then dip a probe in cement and push it in and out of the hole.

Use a needle from the kit to push a piece of cement-coated vulcanized rubber in the hole. Remove needle and trim off excess rubber.

THE RIGHT JACK. Choose the proper jack for your particular situation, whether it is a truck, car, jeep, big tractor, small tractor, or even lawn mower. The right jack can mean the difference between a good safe job and one that will not only drive you up the wall, but can be downright unsafe.

A bumper jack just won't do, unless it is one such as the screw jack shown. This will lift up small tractors and autos, but isn't up to larger stuff. One of the best jacks you can own is a good hydraulic, however these are quite expensive. The main problem with hydraulic jacks is getting them under the item to be lifted. However, when they fit, nothing can be easier to use.

Make sure you use all safety precautions when using the jack. Keep the jack on level ground and make sure it is set under the equipment so it can't slip off. Stand off to one side and clear of the jack when operating it so it can't injure you if it should slip off and "pop" backwards. By all means, never get under a piece of equipment being held by a jack alone. Instead use approved automobile jack stands.

In most instances, unless you live a long distance from a nearby town or service station, you'll be better off having the tire repaired by the "pros" with the right equipment. With the right equipment fixing a flat is nothing, which is why fixing a flat can still be done at bargain prices, even with today's inflation. On the other hand, attempting to fix a flat without equipment is a huge hassle. Getting the tire off the rim on heavy duty farm equipment requires a great deal of effort unless you have specialized tire tools.

Smaller Tires With Tubes

Small tires such as those for garden tractors are a different story, however, and you can use nothing more than a rubber-faced hammer and a couple of large old, blunt screwdrivers for these jobs.

The first step is to use a valve stem remover to remove the inside of the valve stem and allow the tire to completely deflate. Then use the rubber hammer to break the tire bead from the rim. Work

Use the right size jack. This screw jack is ideal for small tractors and light equipment, as is a small hydraulic jack.

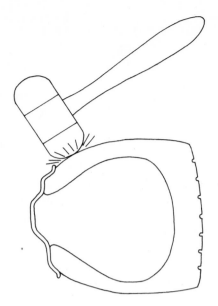

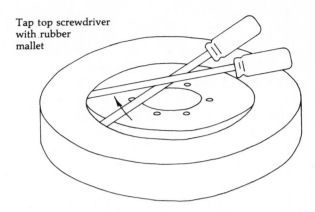

Tap top screwdriver with rubber mallet

To remove the tire from the rim, first break the bead by deflating the tire and striking the edge with a rubber mallet. Then work two screwdrivers as shown to pry the tire off the rim.

around the tire a little at a time. The rubber faced hammer reduces the chance of damaging the tire rim. Turn the tire over and break the bead on the other side in the same manner.

Once the bead has been broken you can then push the large screwdriver in behind the edge of the tire and bring it back over the edge of the wheel rim. Now take a second large screwdriver and slip in beside the first. Use the rubber-faced hammer to tap it around the wheel rim and away from the first screwdriver. Hold the first screwdriver in place by standing on it with your foot at the same time.

Once you have one side of the tire removed you can usually reach in and remove the tube.

To locate the hole, inflate the tube and place it in a tank of water. A stream of bubbles indicates where the hole is. Mark the location with a crayon. Then dry off the tire, deflate it and rough up the area around the hole with coarse sandpaper or a metal rasp. Apply tire patching cement to the spot, allow to dry, then apply a cold patch over the cement, after first peeling off the backing paper. Roll firmly in place with a large bolt or other round item, and replace the tube back in the tire.

Position the valve stem through hole in wheel rim, making sure it is straight and

not pinched. Then inflate tire until the beads on both sides "pop" back in place. Warning: Don't inflate too much; and stand back from tire—not directly over it. Replace the valve stem center and inflate to the proper tire pressure.

If necessary, a tubeless tire can be patched in the same method, but one problem is that the tire beads often won't fit up tight enough against the rim to seal and allow you to inflate the tire. One solution is to tie a heavy rope around the tire and twist it "Spanish-windlass" fashion to force the tire down flat and squeeze the beads in place against the wheel rim. Again, leave out the valve stem center until the tire beads pop in place, then place it in and inflate as necessary.

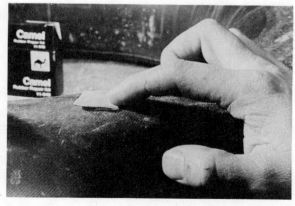

Patch the tube with a standard cold patch once the cement is dry.

114

Index

Other Garden Way Books
You Will Enjoy

The owner/builder and the home-owner concerned about energy conservation and alternate construction methods will find an up-to-date library essential. Here are some excellent books in these areas.

Low-Cost Pole Building Construction, by Doublas Merrilees and Evelyn Loveday. 118 pp., deluxe paperback. $5.95. This will save you money, labor, time and materials.

Build Your Own Stone House, by Karl and Sue Schwenke. 156 pp., quality paperback, $5.95; hardback, $10.95. With their help, you can build your own beautiful stone home.

The Complete Homesteading Book, by David Robinson, 256 pp., quality paperback, $5.95; hardback, $8.95. How to live a simpler, more self-sufficient life.

Build Your Own Low-Cost Log Home, by Roger E. Hard. 204 pages, 8½ × 11, quality paperback, $7.95; cloth, $12.50. A remarkably complete home construction book.

Designing and Building a Solar House, by Donald Watson, 288 pages, 8½ × 11, quality paperback, $9.95; cloth, $12.95. "A nuts-and-bolts book that brings the sun down to earth," said Alvin Toffler, author of **Future Shock.**

Heating with Wood, by Larry Gay. 128 pages, 6 × 8, quality paperback, $3.95. All the basic information you need for switching to wood heat.

Methanol & Other Ways Around the Gas Pump, by John Ware Lincoln. 144 pages; quality paperback, $5.95. How to "drive without gas"—using methanol—and a look at the past experiments and future politics of our gasoline supply.

Homemade: 101 Easy-to-Make Things for Your Garden, Home or Farm, by Ken Braren and Roger Griffith. 176 pages, quality paperback, 8½ × 11, $6.95. Plans and instructions for making fences, chairs, birdhouses, potting benches, and scores of other useful items for country living.

Building the House You Can Afford, by Stu Campbell. 160 pages, 8½ × 11, quality paperback, $9.95; hardcover, $14.95. An illustrated, step-by-step guide to saving up to 20% on construction costs by being your own contractor.

Wood Heat Safety, by Jay Shelton. 176 pp., 8½ × 11, quality paperback, $8.95. The definitive book on safe installation and operation of wood stoves and chimneys, written by an expert in the field. The best book on this subject currently available.

Be Your Own Chimney Sweep, by Chris Curtis and Donald Post. 112 pages, 6 × 9, quality paperback, $4.95. Two professional sweeps tell how to clean stoves, stovepipes and chimneys efficiently and safely.

Wood Energy: A Practical Guide to Heating With Wood, by Mary Twitchell. Quality paperback, 8½ × 11, 176 pages, $7.95. The definitive wood heat book, with comprehensive catalog section on stoves and furnaces.

Home Energy for the Eighties, by Ralph Wolfe and Peter Clegg. Quality paperback, 8½ × 11, 272 pages, $10.95. How to deal with the energy crisis by turning to solar heat, water power, wind power, and wood. Plus illustrated catalog sections on what's available now in these fields.

At Home in the Sun: An Open-House Tour of Solar Homes in the United States, by Norah Davis and Linda Lindsey. Quality paperaback, 8½ × 11, 248 pages, $9.95. What it's really like to live in a solar house, as told by the owners of thirty-one solar homes around the country.

Harnessing Water Power for Home Energy, by Dermot McGuigan. 112 pages, quality paperback, $4.95; hardback $9.95. An authoritative, detailed look at the uses of small-scale water power.

Harnessing Wind Power for Home Energy, by Dermot McGuigan. 144 pages, quality paperback, $4.95; hardback $9.95. A solid, complete analysis of wind power options for homeowners, with details on machines, manufacturers, and whole systems.

These books are available at your bookstore, or directly from Garden Way Publishing, Box 171X, Charlotte, Vermont 05445. If ordering by mail and your order is under $10, please enclose 75¢ for postage and handling.